T0130200

SEEING THE WORLD IN 3-D

DECEPTION, DELUSION, AND
DELIVERANCE IN THE LAST DAYS

DENNY STAHL

WESTBOW
PRESS®
A DIVISION OF THOMAS NELSON
& ZONDERVAN

This book is a work of non-fiction. Unless otherwise noted, the author and the publisher make no explicit guarantees as to the accuracy of the information contained in this book and in some cases, names of people and places have been altered to protect their privacy.

WestBow Press books may be ordered through booksellers or by contacting:

WestBow Press
A Division of Thomas Nelson & Zondervan
1663 Liberty Drive
Bloomington, IN 47403
www.westbowpress.com
844-714-3454

All Scripture quotations are taken from the New King James Version. Copyright © 1982 by Thomas Nelson, Inc. Used by permission. All rights reserved.

ISBN: 979-8-3850-1503-0 (sc)
ISBN: 979-8-3850-1504-7 (e)

Library of Congress Control Number: 2023924256

Print information available on the last page.

WestBow Press rev. date: 02/22/2024

DEDICATION

This book is dedicated to my personal Lord and Savior, Jesus Christ, who gave me the lens of scripture and the power of the Holy Spirit so that my blind natural eyes were opened to see the One who is the way, the truth, and the life.

PREFACE

We certainly live in interesting times, don't we? Bombarded daily and constantly by information that seems to come from every direction and through all kinds of media, all sounding authoritative and accurate and making demands on us to take a stand for the "truth." What used to be seen as debate has become a shouting match with the decibel level of the noise reaching deafening levels. Accusations about "misinformation" come from every side of every issue, and the efforts to "cancel" ideas and perspectives and even people have become the rage. In this hostile, uptight, angry culture, you may find it increasingly difficult to decide whom to trust, and what to believe. This book is written for anyone interested in truly developing an ability to see clearly through the fog so that he or she will be able to navigate the highway of life successfully without being distracted or diverted from the course God wants you to take.

ACKNOWLEDGEMENTS

First and foremost, I want to thank my beautiful bride, Vickie, for encouraging me every step along the way as I developed and authored this book. My love for the Bible, the whole counsel of God, and my love for the truth, the whole truth, and nothing but the truth was spawned by my pastor, Chuck Smith. I still have boxes of notes that I took while attending his Bible studies at Calvary Chapel Costa Mesa. He took his congregation through ten chapters a week in his studies of the Old Testament, and through five chapters a week in his studies through the New Testament. I will never forget his in-depth studies through the books of Daniel, Romans, and Revelation. In addition, I am grateful for the teachings of Pastor Jon Courson. During the years I served at the Applegate Christian Fellowship, Jon gave me opportunities in a wide range of ministry that helped mold me into who I am today. I also want to thank the members of the Applegate Christian Fellowship, Canyonville Bible Academy, Yreka Bible Church, Deschutes Christian Fellowship, and Calvary Chapel Grants Pass for allowing me the blessed privilege of pastoring them, serving them, and teaching them the Bible through many dangers, trials, and years of fruitfulness. I am deeply indebted to our dear friends, Dave and Luci Wurch, and Robert and Jocelyn Husel, for their love and financial support.

CONTENTS

SECTION 3 - DELIVERANCE

INTRODUCTION

These difficult days and our perplexing problems have many wondering about the very same issue on the minds of a group of twelve men in Jerusalem two thousand years ago. They had just heard an extraordinary and puzzling statement by the man they had been following regarding the huge hand-hewn stones used in the construction of their temple. As they all reached the end of the arduous climb from the Garden of Gethsemane to the summit on the Mount of Olives and stopped to rest, they approached him privately and asked him three questions: "Tell us, when will these things be? And what will be the sign of Your coming, and of the end of the age?"[1] And Jesus answered and said to them: "Take heed that no one deceives you. For many will come in My name, saying, 'I am the Christ,' and will deceive many. Then many false prophets will rise up and deceive many. For false christs and false prophets will rise and show great signs and wonders to deceive, if possible, even the elect."[2] Repeatedly, in response to their inquiry regarding the coming destruction of the Jewish Temple, His second coming, and the end of the age, Jesus warned His very own disciples about their vulnerability to deception. Why was Jesus so adamant about warning them about their vulnerability to deception? Jesus was equipping His disciples for the battles they were about to face in an invisible war that would bring about a continuing progression of deception. Please note that these men were the "A" postles, not the "B" postels, they were the ones He had personally picked to take the message of the gospel to the ends of the earth, and if Jesus was concerned about their vulnerability to deception, I am sure that He is concerned about our own vulnerability to deception! We all need to be equipped to distinguish the difference between what is true, and what is false, what is fact, and what is fiction. Why? Because of how difficult that is going to become in the future.

I will never forget the first movie I saw in 3-D. *The Mask* was somewhat of a hit in movie theaters partly due to the novelty of "you must put on the mask," referring to those cumbersome glasses everyone in the audience had to put on during the four 3-D sequences in the film. Thanks to James Cameron and Steven Spielberg, 3-D movies are back in a big way. James Cameron released his movie, *Avatar* in 3-D in 2009 and audiences around the world were in awe of the other-worldly scenery and spectacular special effects. Walt Disney Studios followed suit in 2010 when they released the third installment in the Chronicles of Narnia, *The Voyage of the Dawn Treader*, in 3-D in 2010. Pixar animation studios retooled a 2003 mega-hit and re-released the movie *Finding Nemo* in 3-D in 2012. And in 2015, the final movie in the Peter Jackson trilogy, *The Hobbit*, was released worldwide in 3-D. And 3-D is not restricted to motion pictures. In 2010, ESPN launched its broadcast of live sporting events in 3-D. Today, satellite TV providers like Direct TV offer several channels of 3-D programming. The trouble is you must wear special 3-D glasses and the special glasses, and the 3-D television set are not cheap.

What I want to propose to you is absolutely free. All that is required is your willingness to travel with me through the pages of this book so that we may all be able to see the world in 3-D. We do not need special glasses or tv sets to be able to see the deception, delusion, and deliverance that is right in front of us. First, we will investigate deception; second, we will uncover delusion; and third, we will discover deliverance.

SECTION 1

DECEPTION

What is deception? The *Merriam-Webster Collegiate Dictionary* defines *deception* as

1
a: the act of causing someone to accept as true or valid what is false or invalid: the act of deceiving
b: the fact or condition of being deceived

2: something that deceives: trick.[3]

We all have a certain fascination when it comes to deception. Anyone who has witnessed a card trick using sleight of hand or the seemingly impossible feats of magic performed by illusionists knows that there is some trick—some unknown facts—that defy our senses, logic, and understanding. But I promise you, I have nothing up my sleeve. Besides, like Rocky and Bullwinkle, I know that trick never works. So, we will look at deception as an intellectual/scientific phenomenon, as a social/economic phenomenon, and as a spiritual/religious phenomenon.

CHAPTER 1

UNMASKING THE DECEIVER

HIS IDENTITY

THERE IS DANGER LURKING IN an invisible dimension that we must expose. The apostle Paul warned Timothy that deception in these last days would be delivered by a deceiver. We must pull the mask off the deceiver and expose his agents and their agenda in these last days. As Paul explained to the believers in Corinth, "Lest Satan should take advantage of us; for we are not ignorant of his devices."[4] Paul was certain of something I believe few of us are so sure about. Do we truly understand the devices of the devil? Sadly, many do not even believe that Satan is real!

Thankfully, the Bible is the source for our understanding of this malevolent being. It is found in the beginning of that remarkable resource, the book of Genesis. In the third chapter, we are introduced to a new character who seems to come out of nowhere, a malignant being who is immediately revealed as the bitter enemy of both God and the newly created man and woman: "Now the serpent was more cunning than any beast of the field which the Lord God had made."[5]

Who is this being, and where did he come from? At first, he is described as a serpent, and to dispel any doubt as to the identity of the animating mind and voice that spoke then, we have the clear, unmistakable identification at the end of the Bible, where we read: "So the great dragon was cast out, that serpent of old, called the Devil and Satan, who deceives the whole world; he was cast to the earth, and his angels were cast out with him."[6]

We should consider the origin of this evil being and thus find the answer to the great question of the origin of sin. The knowledge of those facts should enable us to align our thinking with God's regarding the current conflicts in a world beset by perplexing problems. This should bring us to a clearer picture of our future, which is overcast with danger and difficulties unprecedented in human history. As we prosecute our case against this malevolent being, we will be dependent on the Holy Spirit to lead us into all truth. We will rely on the Word of God, as it recorded Satan's beginning as a created being, his sin and rebellion against God, his diabolical schemes against God and humanity, and his fate at the hands of the Judge of the universe.

The Bible describes the prehistory of this fallen spirit being: "How you are fallen from heaven, O Lucifer, son of the morning. How you are cut down to the ground, you who weakened the nations! For you have said in your heart: 'I will ascend into heaven, I will exalt my throne above the stars of God; I will also sit on the mount of the congregation on the farthest sides of the north; I will ascend above the heights of the clouds, I will be like the Most High.' Yet you shall be brought down to Sheol, to the lowest depths of the Pit."[7]

The ancient Hebrew prophet Ezekiel was given a word from the Lord that gives us a glimpse into the very origin of sin:

> Moreover the word of the Lord came to me, saying, "Son of man, take up a lamentation for the king of Tyre, and say to him, 'Thus says the Lord God: You were the seal of perfection, full of wisdom and perfect in beauty. You were in Eden,

the garden of God; every precious stone was your covering: the sardius, topaz, and diamond, beryl, onyx, and jasper, sapphire, turquoise, and emerald with gold. The workmanship of your timbrels and pipes was prepared for you on the day you were created. You were the anointed cherub who covers; I established you; you were on the holy mountain of God; you walked back and forth in the midst of fiery stones. You were perfect in your ways from the day you were created, till iniquity was found in you. By the abundance of your trading, you became filled with violence within, and you sinned; Therefore I cast you as a profane thing out of the mountain of God; and I destroyed you, O covering cherub, from the midst of the fiery stones.'"[8]

Suffice it to say that from these passages we learn that there was a time in eternity past when evil did not exist. This lovely spirit creature, Lucifer, which means "Star of the Morning," was lifted with pride, sinned within himself, and rebelled against his Maker. We are not told when this original sin occurred, and to that question there is much debate, but I believe it was sometime before God set in motion His plan of the ages concerning the glory of His only begotten Son, Jesus Christ.

God initiated that plan sometime during a phase in creation when the earth was without form and void: "In the beginning God created the heavens and the earth. The earth was without form, and void; and darkness *was* on the face of the deep. And the Spirit of God was hovering over the face of the waters."[9] Please notice the period at the end of the first sentence: Hebrew scholars tell us that the first verse of Genesis is a complete thought. So, how did the earth become without form and void, Denny? Great question. There is a verse in Isaiah that plainly reveals to us that God did not create it so: "For thus says the Lord, who created the heavens, who is God, who formed the earth and made it, who has established it, who did not create it in vain, who formed it to be inhabited: 'I *am* the Lord, and *there is* no other.'"[10] The Hebrew scriptures are much clearer—the Hebrew word translated here as "in vain" is the same Hebrew word used in Genesis 1:2 (there translated "without form and void"). The careful reader of the first chapter of Genesis will note that the word "create" is found in the first verse and is not used again until the introduction of animate life in the fifth and sixth days of creation. God was not simply using literary effect when He used the words "created the heavens," "formed the earth," "and made it," "who has established it," and "who formed it to be inhabited." To create is to produce something out of nothing; it is to call into existence some material thing without using anything already in existence. It is the materialization of a creative thought of the one and only living God. The other verbs which Moses used to describe the work of the six days, such as "made," "divide," and "set," are used elsewhere in the Bible of work done with existing materials. Thus, the Lord God created the heavens and earth—not "without form and void"—and then, as described in Genesis and in Isaiah, He formed and made it, established it, and prepared it for human habitation after it had become "without form and void."

HIS HISTORY WITH HUMANITY

And it was when God created man and woman that the deceiver targeted humanity—perhaps because God created humanity in His own likeness, something that He did not do when He created the angels. The Bible records for us that, on various occasions, God spoke to Satan through the agency that Satan had used to invade the realm of humans. The first time we are introduced to Satan is recorded for us in Genesis 3:13–15, when Satan used the serpent as his intermediary: "And the Lord God said to the woman, 'What *is* this you have done?' The woman said, 'The serpent deceived me, and I ate.' So, the Lord God said to the serpent: 'Because you have done this, you *are* cursed more than all cattle, and more than every beast of the field; on your belly you shall go, and you shall eat dust all the days of your life.'"[11] Let's pause for one second and realize that here in verse 14, the Lord God is cursing the agent, the snake, not the antagonist, Satan. Now let's read verse 15: "And I will put enmity between you and the woman, and between your seed and her Seed; He shall bruise your head, and you shall bruise His heel."[12] Please notice that in verse 15, the Lord God spoke through the agent and addressed the antagonist directly, outlining the articles of war, the rules of engagement, and the ultimate outcome of the conflict. Please note that the Lord God said, "I will put enmity between you and the woman." It was God who put hatred, both holy and unholy, into the conflict, which has raged across six thousand years of human history. Satan hates his Creator and humanity with an unholy hatred. Since the fall, every human is born with a nature that is at war with God and terrified of death, and thus subject to bondage. And God hates sin with a holy hatred whenever it is found in any of His creatures. It is against this black background of hatred that the love of God shines even more brilliantly. The hatred placed by God between Satan and humanity was especially marked in its outpouring from Satan against the Son of Man, the Lord Jesus Christ.

Thousands of years after that first encounter recorded for us in Genesis, the gospels reveal that Jesus spoke directly to Satan through the agent Satan had used to rebuke the Lord even when it was Peter, one of the Lord's disciples: "But He turned and said to Peter, 'Get behind Me, Satan! You are an offense to Me, for you are not mindful of the things of God, but the things of men.'"[13] Once again, Satan, the antagonist, had invaded the human realm and spoke through an agent – this time not the serpent, but Peter the apostle. Jesus, alert to the reality of what had just happened, rebuked Peter for his having been deceived, and taught His disciples a valuable lesson in spiritual warfare.

For a moment, put yourself in Peter's sandals. Prior to being rebuked by Jesus, Peter had been commended by Jesus for Peter's answer to the question Jesus had posed to all His apostles: "Who do you say I am?"[14] After Peter's answer, "You are the Christ, the Son of the living God,"[15] Jesus commended Peter and told Peter the source of his answer: "Flesh and blood has not revealed this to you, but My Father who is in heaven."[16] Jesus congratulated Peter for having his mind tuned to a heavenly frequency to receive revelation from God Almighty. In other words, it was not Peter's natural ability to observe and identify that produced his answer concerning Jesus' identity, but supernatural revelation from an invisible source. Then, Peter must have allowed his mind to wander to a different frequency and a far different invisible source when he issued his stern rebuke to Jesus' prophecy concerning His coming arrest, trial, and crucifixion in Jerusalem. Let Peter's experience be an example to all of us. We have the capacity to receive information and inspiration that come from invisible realms – one heavenly in origin – and the other demonic and deceptive in origin. Thinkers and speakers beware. It's like the old radio receiver in my dad's Chevrolet – you had to turn the dial ever so carefully to avoid the static and tune successfully into the correct frequency of your favorite radio station to be able to hear their broadcast clearly.

HIS 1ST VICTIM - EVE

It is our intention to pull the mask off the deceiver and expose his diabolical, deceptive, and destructive history. The Bible records for us the occasion of his first victim: "And the Lord God said to the woman, 'What *is* this you have done?' The woman said, 'The serpent deceived me, and I ate.'"[17] Paul the apostle affirmed this fact: "And Adam was not deceived, but the woman being deceived, fell into transgression."[18] The Bible never holds Eve responsible for what happened next. The Bible is clear about who is responsible for the entrance of sin and death into the world: "Therefore, just as through *one man* sin entered the world."[19], "by the *one man's* offense many died"[20] "by the *one man's* offense death reigned"[21] But the deception of Eve played a role in the Adam Bomb.

SATAN'S DEVICES

So, let's try to de-construct what happened to Eve in order that we might be equipped to recognize the dangers of deception – and how deception works. The Bible records for us what took place:

> Now the serpent was more cunning than any beast of the field which the Lord God had made. And he said to the woman, "Has God indeed said, 'You shall not eat of every tree of the garden'?" And the woman said to the serpent, "We may eat the fruit of the trees of the garden; but of the fruit of the tree which *is* in the midst of the garden, God has said, 'You shall not eat it, nor shall you touch it, lest you die.'" Then the serpent said to the woman, "You will not surely die. For God knows that in the day you eat of it your eyes will be opened, and you will be like God, knowing good and evil." So, when the woman saw that the tree *was* good for food, that it *was* pleasant to the eyes, and a tree desirable to make *one* wise, she took of its fruit and ate. She also gave to her husband with her, and he ate.[22]

Now, I want to focus your attention – not on the results of her deception, but on the process of her deception. Let's focus on the deceiver's clever tactics. First, he asks Eve a subtle question of doubt concerning the authenticity and validity of God's instructions to humanity: "Has God indeed said, 'You shall not eat of every tree of the garden'?" Doubt and ignorance come from Satan and not from God who alone is the source of certainty and knowledge. We may be sure that any questioning of the Word of God is Satanic in its origin. Whether the doubt is raised by a group of atheists, by secular educators, by theologians, or by ministers, its source is always the same. Second, he tells Eve an outright lie: "You will not surely die." That is an outright lie. Third, Satan made a subtle suggestion: "For God knows that in the day you eat of it your eyes will be opened, and you will be like God, knowing good and evil." In other words, Satan suggested to Eve that God was withholding something from her, that He was not to be trusted, that she should be His equal. Satan cast doubt, lied, and made Satanic suggestions and Eve succumbed.

EVE'S MISTAKES

Why did Eve give in to Satan's clever and subtle deceptions? She made six critical errors. She erred in mishandling the Word of God, and she erred in her misperceptions. Please notice that three times Eve mishandled the Word of God. First, she responded to the serpent's subtle question of doubt and omitted something from God's Word when she said: "We may eat the fruit of the trees of the garden." Please compare Eve's statement to what God said. Please look at Genesis 2:16: "And the Lord God commanded the man, saying, 'Of every tree of the garden you may freely eat;'" Notice any difference to what God had said to what Eve stated in her response to the serpent? Eve omitted something from what God said, she omitted "freely." God had commanded Adam to eat "freely" of every tree. Eve's first error was omitting something from God's Word. Second, she added to God's Word. Please notice she added something God never said: "nor shall you touch it." Not only did she omit God's Word, and add to God's Word, but she also changed God's Word. She changed God's Word when she said, "lest you die." Please take another look at Genesis 2:16-17: Notice any difference to what God had said to what Eve stated in her response to the serpent? Eve changed something that God had said. God had declared that in the day that you eat of it "you shall surely die." Eve's third error was changing God's Word. That is when, seeing and seizing on Eve's vulnerability to deception, Satan launched his outright lie in her direction: "You will not surely die. For God knows that in the day you eat of it your eyes will be opened, and you will be like God, knowing good and evil."

That is when Satan's doubt -filled question and outright lie, mixed with Eve's three errors in mishandling the Word of God, altered Eve's perceptions. It is right there in verse 6: "So when the woman saw that the tree *was* good for food, that it *was* pleasant to the eyes, and a tree desirable to make *one* wise, ..." Please note the three things that Eve saw, her three misperceptions. First, she saw that the tree was good for food. What a mistake. A fatal mistake. Was the tree "good for food"? The lust of the flesh now dominated her thinking. Second, she saw that the tree was pleasant to the eyes. What a mistake. A fatal mistake. Was the tree "pleasant to the eyes"? The lust of the eyes now dominated her thinking. Third, she saw that the tree was desirable to make one wise. What a mistake. A fatal mistake. Was the tree "desirable to make one wise"? The pride of life now dominated her thinking. That is when Satan's doubt-filled question and outright lie, mixed with Eve's three errors in mishandling the Word of God, and Eve's mistaken perceptions, led to her misguided conduct. It is right there in the rest of verse 6: "she took of its fruit and ate. She also gave to her husband with her, and he ate." First, she was no longer submitted to God. She was in control of herself, independent of God and, so "she took of its fruit." Second, "she ate" - her sense of control led to her consuming the forbidden fruit. Third, "she gave" – not completely content with her sense of control, and yet satisfied that her consuming of the fruit had not led to the consequences God had warned her about, she then conveyed the forbidden fruit to her husband. She was not yet conscious of the fact that she had been deceived.

Thousands of years later, Satan tempted Jesus in a similar way after Jesus had fasted for forty days in the wilderness. Please note that Satan's methods had not changed. Satan appealed to and tried to exploit the Messiah's desperate need for food when Satan suggested that Jesus miraculously change stones into bread to satisfy His physical needs. But Jesus resisted Satan's appeal to the lusts of the flesh as He declared, "It is written, 'Man shall not live by bread alone, but by every word that proceeds from the mouth of God.' "[23] Then Satan tried to appeal to the pride of life when he took Jesus to the pinnacle of the Temple in Jerusalem, and after quoting verses from Psalm 91, Satan dared Jesus to demonstrate His deity by throwing Himself down off the heights of the Temple into the valley below. Jesus declared: "It is written again, 'You shall not tempt the LORD your God.'"[24] Finally, Satan appealed to the lust of the eyes when he took Jesus to a lofty perch on a high mountain and showed Jesus all the kingdoms of the world and their glory and offered all of it to Jesus if Jesus would only "bow down and worship me." Jesus did not dispute Satan's right to grant the kingdoms of the world to whomsoever he wished, but stated: "Away with you, Satan! For it is written, 'You shall worship the LORD your God, and Him only you shall serve.'"[25] Please note that in all three of His responses to the three temptations of Satan Jesus quoted from a portion of the Book of Deuteronomy Chapter 6. Jesus repelled Satan's temptation by remembering and quoting Scripture. Like King David wrote, "Your word I have hidden in my heart, that I might not sin against You."[26] What a perfect example this encounter is for us today just as the apostle John wrote: "Do not love the world or the things in the world. If anyone loves the world, the love of the Father is not in him. For all that *is* in the world—the lust of the flesh, the lust of the eyes, and the pride of life—is not of the Father but is of the world. And the world is passing away, and the lust of it; but he who does the will of God abides forever. These things I have written to you concerning those who *try to* deceive you."[27]

THE RESULTS

The results of Eve's deception are recorded for us in Genesis 3:7-13: "Then the eyes of both of them were opened, and they knew that they *were* naked; and they sewed fig leaves together and made themselves coverings. And they heard the sound of the Lord God walking in the garden in the cool of the day, and Adam and his wife hid themselves from the presence of the Lord God among the trees of the garden."[28] Thus, Eve unwittingly became the conduit of corruption, as is revealed beginning in verse seven and verse eight. Suddenly and immediately, just as God had warned, the consequences of disobedience overtook their rebellion. Adam and Eve were ek-chabad – the glory of God which had covered their physical nakedness vanished, and in a vain effort to cover their guilt and shame, they camouflaged themselves and tried to hide from God among the trees in the garden.

But God intervened in their foolishness:

> Then the Lord God called to Adam and said to him, "Where *are* you?" So he said, "I heard Your voice in the garden, and I was afraid because I was naked; and I hid myself." And He said, "Who told you that you *were* naked? Have you eaten from the tree of which I commanded you that you should

not eat?" Then the man said, "The woman whom You gave *to be* with me, she gave me of the tree, and I ate." And the Lord God said to the woman, "What *is* this you have done?" The woman said, "The serpent deceived me, and I ate."[29]

Afraid, they both ran from God, hid themselves, and improvised a man-made covering for their nakedness. When the Lord overtook Adam, and asked him the reason for his flight, a second result of his sin was immediately seen. Man had become a coward and a liar. Instead of honestly confessing his sin, Adam blamed his wife, and he blamed God for giving her to him! Thus, in the articles of the invisible war, God determined that fear, cowardice, and deceit were to disturb humanity so long as they continued in rebellion.

Up to this moment, Adam had enjoyed blessed fellowship with His Creator and received an assignment from His Maker. It was sort of, *God & son, Inc.* in the garden of Eden. God had bequeathed authority and dominion over all the earth to Adam; but now in his rebellion, Adam had unwittingly relinquished that role to the one to whom he had yielded himself. Now the conditions of work were changed dramatically for Adam, as in the sweat of his brow he would till the soil to cultivate nature to provide food for his sustenance. Please note that Jesus Christ recognized the usurped authority that Satan now wielded when He called Satan "the ruler of this world."[30]

Oh, what wreck and ruin the Deceiver has brought to human history! Repeatedly and relentlessly, he has used deception successfully in every arena of life. Sadly, the Evil One has partnered with demons, men, and women, and taught his deceptive ways to any and all who would participate in his evil agenda.

CHAPTER 2

DECEPTION IN THE INTELLECTUAL, SCIENTIFIC REALM

Now that we have pulled the mask of the deceiver, let's consider deception in the intellectual, scientific realm.

THE HEAVENS ARE SPEAKING TO US

4,000 years ago, King David wrote: "The heavens declare the glory of God; and the firmament shows His handiwork. Day unto day utters speech, and night unto night reveals knowledge. *There is* no speech nor language *where* their voice is not heard. Their line has gone out through all the earth, and their words to the end of the world." [31]

Indeed, the heavens have been speaking to us and just since 1931 we have been listening intently via the discovery and development of radio astronomy and the construction of vast arrays of radio telescopes which are pointed to the heavens all around the world listening and mapping outer space according to the "speech" we continue to attempt to decipher. In addition to listening to their words which have gone out to the whole world, we have the technology today to send an optical telescope beyond the impediment of earth's atmosphere and when it is in need of repair we have intercepted it as it orbits the earth, carefully captured it, and sent astronauts on space walks to conduct difficult, delicate tasks to repair and update its systems so that it may send us stunning photos of the universe.

Despite this research, the scientific community's investigation of our universe has already been corrupted by their adherence to the theory of evolution. According to Northrop Gruman's website:

> The Hubble Space Telescope can show us what the universe looked like billions of years before our ancestors crawled out of the ocean and on to dry land. But to seek out our cosmic origins from light emitted at the very dawn of the universe, astronomers need an observatory dedicated to operating in the infrared spectrum where that light can be detected. Furthermore, using spectrographic instruments to split incoming light into its constituent wavelengths, scientists can explore the atmospheres and characteristics of distant alien planets, a crucial component of finding planets that support extraterrestrial life like ours.

On Christmas Day, 2021, NASA launched the Next Generation Space Telescope, named for astronomer James C. Webb which arrived in January 2022 at the Sun-Earth position it now occupies. The first image from the telescope was released to the public via a press conference on July 11, 2022. The images are stunningly beautiful like the one taken of the Carina Nebula called "Cosmic Cliffs" by NASA.

When you look up into the night sky, how many stars do you see? Hubble has discovered that many of those points of light that we would describe as individual stars are galaxies. Research has confirmed that each galaxy consists of millions of individual stars. Throughout history, humanity has tried to count the stars we observe in the night sky. In 128 BC, Hipparchus confidently declared that there were 1,026. In 1600, Keppler confidently declared that there were a mere 1,005. In 2003, astronomers estimated that according to their calculations, there must be seventy sextillions!

NEWTON'S MODEL OF THE SOLAR SYSTEM

One of the greatest scientists of all time, Sir Isaac Newton once said, "A man may imagine things that are false, but he can only understand things that are true, for if the things be false, the apprehension of them is not understanding."

Newton had a replica of our solar system made in miniature. In the center was the sun with its retinue of planets revolving around it. A scientist entered Newton's study one day, and exclaimed, "My, what an exquisite thing this is. Who made it?" "Nobody." replied Newton to the questioner who was an unbeliever. "You must think I am a fool. Of course, somebody made it, and he is a genius." Laying his book aside, Newton arose and laid a hand on his friend's shoulder and said: "This thing is but a puny imitation of a much grander system whose laws you and I know, and I am not able to convince you that this mere toy is without a designer and maker; yet you profess to believe that the great original from which the design is taken has come into being without either designer or maker. Now tell me, by what sort of reasoning do you reach such incongruous conclusions?"

KING DAVID'S AND SIR JOHANNES KEPLER'S STATEMENTS

King David wrote:

> When I consider Your heavens, the work of Your fingers, the moon and the stars, which You have ordained, what is man that You are mindful of him, and the son of man that You visit him? For You have made him a little lower than the angels, and You have crowned him with glory and honor. You have made him to have dominion over the works of Your hands; You have put all *things* under his feet, all sheep and oxen — even the beasts of the field, the birds of the air, and the fish of the sea that pass through the paths of the seas.[32]

The scientific community should take heed to the observation King David made about being humbled by the incredible diversity and complexity visible in outer space and in inner space, and echoed by the statement by one of the most revered scientists in history, Sir Johannes Kepler: "The chief aim of all investigations of the external world should be to discover the rational order and harmony which has been imposed upon it by God."[33] My, how that definition of science has been abandoned and mocked within the academic community of today!

DR. JOB MARTIN'S *INCREDIBLE CREATURES THAT DEFY EVOLUTION*

We are grateful for Exploration Films' DVD series, *Incredible Creatures That Defy Evolution*, featuring Dr. Job Martin. Martin himself was a traditional evolutionist, but his medical and scientific training would go through a revolution when he began to study animals that challenged the scientific assumptions of his education.

BOMBARDIER BEETLE

One of the creatures that caught his attention was the bombardier beetle. "If there is any creature on earth that could not possibly have evolved, that creature is the Bombardier Beetle. It needed God to create it with all its systems fully functional."

The study of this incredible insect has been going on for many years. In 1928, authors C. L. Metcalf and R. L. Flint wrote: 'The bombardier beetle, Brachinus, ejects an acrid fluid which is discharged with a distinct popping sound and a small cloud of vapor that looks like the smoke from a miniature cannon.'"[34]

More recently, Time magazine reports: "The bombardier (beetle) does appear to be unique in the animal kingdom. Its defense system is extraordinarily intricate, a cross between tear gas and a tommy gun. When the beetle senses danger, it internally mixes enzymes contained in one body chamber with concentrated solutions of some rather harmless compounds, hydrogen peroxide and hydroquinones, confined to a second chamber. This generates a noxious spray of caustic benzoquinones, which explodes from its body at a boiling 212°F. What is more, the fluid is pumped through twin rear nozzles, which can be rotated, like a B-17's gun turret, to hit a hungry ant or frog with bull's eye accuracy."[35]

In response to the article in Time magazine, the Institute For Creation Research wrote:

> The bombardier beetle does appear to be unique in the animal kingdom. Its defense system is extraordinarily intricate, a cross between tear gas and a Tommy gun. When the beetle senses

danger, it internally mixes enzymes contained in one body chamber with concentrated solutions of some rather harmless compounds, hydrogen peroxide [the same used as fuel for the rockets to space flights] and hydroquinones, confined to a second chamber. this generated a noxious spray of caustic benzoquinones, which explodes from its body (*we now know thanks to very high-speed cameras it actually send many mini-explosions very rapidly that we hear it as but one, which would make the beetle itself to be propelled in the opposite direction for every action there's an opposite but equal reaction remember?*) What's more, the fluid is pumped through twin rear nozzles which can be rotated, like a B 17's gun turret, to hit a hungry ant or frog with bull's-eye accuracy. The Bombardier beetle has three separated bladders or containers, two of which contains a neutral chemical. Both, in time of danger, release part of the contents into a "Mixing Chamber" which has some strong muscular walls that contracts, sending this now mixed and deadly chemical, in a machine gun bursts, out twin turrets, that can shout out to 6 feet in a 360 degree pattern, including even forwards, by lifting up its body and shooting underneath itself forwards. Now if this life-form needed to rely upon evolution's billions of years of time to fully develop all these separate systems, they'd be frog lunches, millions of years ago. No, they MUST be Created as they are today, for within the extensive fossil records, there is not half of this and half of that life form, anywhere. Nobody has ever found any part of this 1/2 inch long beetle that fits within the long time evolution ideas, that would have allowed it to live long enough to reproduce itself let alone live period. Not only does this beetle manufacture two chemicals but also a third, an "inhibitor", and it mixes it with the reactive chemical however with this inhibitor the little bug makes it would not be able to use the expulsion of hot, burning liquid and gases to ward off enemies. A spider would kill and eat it as it would have no defense nor a solution to protect itself, and dead beetles cannot evolve. But that chemical turns out to be an anti-inhibitor. When the anti-inhibitor is added to the other chemicals, an explosive reaction does occur and the beetle is able to defend itself. So how many chemicals can this bug make? How does all evolve one step million years apart? What does YOUR common sense tell YOU? SO WHICH SYSTEM of belief or faith in it best explains this little beetle. Creation or evolution? BOTH REQUIRE FAITH, one in God and the other in men. We, each must choose which we have faith in.[36]

PACIFIC GOLDEN PLOVER

A little bird caught Dr. Martin's attention, too. The bird is the Pacific Golden Plover. The 7-ounce bird migrates from Hawaii to Alaska to lay its' eggs, gorges itself for the return flight – it cannot swim – and then leaves its baby birds and flies eighty-eight hours nonstop back to Hawaii. To conserve energy, the plovers exchange position as they fly in formation all the way back to Hawaii. But mom and dad depart before their babies are able to fly with them. Abandoned in Alaska, the baby birds eat and grow and then fly to

Hawaii and arrive about two weeks after their parents. Evolution cannot explain how these little birds developed these amazing habits of procreation.

PAUL'S WARNINGS

Paul the apostle warned Timothy to protect the truth against what some would call "science": "O Timothy! Guard what was committed to your trust, avoiding the profane *and* idle babblings and contradictions of what is falsely called knowledge—by professing it some have strayed concerning the faith." [37] Paul had already written about those who deny their Creator and get caught up in an ever-downward vortex of sin and folly:

> For the wrath of God is revealed from heaven against all ungodliness and unrighteousness of men, who suppress the truth in unrighteousness, because what may be known of God is manifest in them, for God has shown *it* to them. For since the creation of the world His invisible *attributes* are clearly seen, being understood by the things that are made, *even* His eternal power and Godhead, so that they are without excuse, because, although they knew God, they did not glorify *Him* as God, nor were thankful, but became futile in their thoughts, and their foolish hearts were darkened. Professing to be wise, they became fools, and changed the glory of the incorruptible God into an image made like corruptible man—and birds and four-footed animals and creeping things. Therefore God also gave them up to uncleanness, in the lusts of their hearts, to dishonor their bodies among themselves, who exchanged the truth of

God for the lie, and worshiped and served the creature rather than the Creator, who is blessed forever. Amen. [38]

Oh, what wreck and ruin the Deceiver has brought to human history! But, as we have seen, the Evil One has had help. There are those "who suppress the truth in unrighteousness" and there are those "who exchanged the truth of God for the lie." Sadly, many of those individuals call themselves Christians, as an article published online by The Slate titled *Creativity for the Creationist* articulates:

> Forty percent of Americans are evangelical Christians, and many of them reject evolution. Jeff Hardin, chairman of the University of Wisconsin's zoology department, takes this personally. Hardin is an evangelical, but much of his evangelism is directed at his fellow believers. He wants to persuade them that evolution and Christianity are compatible. Today, Hardin speaks for an emerging school of Christian thinkers. They call themselves evolutionary creationists. They believe that God authored the emergence of life and humankind but that evolution explains how this process unfolded. They accept what science has established: The Earth is billions of years old, and all species, including ours, have evolved from other species. Hardin wants evangelicals to trust God. If God made the world, they shouldn't be afraid to see his creation as it is. Hardin approaches science with serene faith. He believes that the evidence he encounters—what Francis Bacon called the 'Book of God's Works' —will be compatible with the Bible. Hardin recognizes, crucially, that when the

two books don't seem to match, the error might be in his own understanding of the Bible. Rather than reject what science has discovered, he asks how scripture can be understood better so that it fits the scientific evidence. [39]

Paul the apostle was aware of the danger of deception in the life of someone who professes to be a believer when he wrote to his disciple, Timothy, and warned him: "Now the Spirit expressly says that in latter times some will depart from the faith, giving heed to deceiving spirits and doctrines of demons, speaking lies in hypocrisy, having their own conscience seared with a hot iron," [40] The impossibility of agreement between the creation narrative and the theory of evolution has been acknowledged by many scientists, including a research scientist with a PhD. from Harvard Medical School who wrote: "When Darwin scientifically rejected the view of species' fixity, many atheists saw the design of life replaced by evolution and, therefore, the Designer replaced by mindless natural processes. Atheism and evolution went hand in hand." [41] He concluded: "In short, atheistic evolution leads to philosophical incoherence. Theistic evolution doesn't fare much better. In the United States, professing Christians are among the most vocal proponents of this view. Yet, the contradictions between evolution and the Bible are stark. It's not possible to harmonize a plain, straightforward reading of the Bible with evolution." [42] In his book, *The Face That Demonstrates the Farce of Evolution*, Hank Hanegraaf identified the belief in theistic evolution as a cruel mistake:

> Under the banner of "theistic evolution" a growing number of Christians maintain that God used evolution as His method of creation. This, in my estimation, is the worst of all possibilities. It is one thing to believe in evolution, it is quite

another to blame God for it. Not only is theistic evolution a contradiction in terms – like the phrase *flaming snowflakes* – but it is also the cruelest, most inefficient system for creation imaginable. As Jacque Monod put it: "[Natural] selection is the blindest, and most cruel way of evolving new species...The struggle for life and the elimination of the weakest is a horrible process, against which our whole modern ethic revolts." An omnipotent, omniscient God does not have to painfully plod through millions of mistakes, misfits, and mutations in order to have fellowship with humans. Rather, He can create humans in a microsecond. If theistic evolution is true, Genesis is at best an allegory and at worst a farce. And if Genesis is an allegory or a farce, the rest of the Bible becomes irrelevant.[43]

EXPOSING EVOLUTION

We are going to pull the mask off the deception behind EVOLUTION. Evolution is not fact, but a theory. It is racist. It is sexist. It sounds liberating, but proves to be, in fact, enslaving. As we shall see, the theory of evolution has spawned racism, genocide, the Holocaust, euthanasia, the sexual revolution, abortion, transhumanism, and AIDS.

ASTRONOMY - THE UNIVERSE HAD A BEGINNING - THE UNIVERSE IS FINE-TUNED FOR LIFE

Have you ever asked the question, "Why is there something rather than nothing?" Have you ever asked the question, "Why is there order rather than chaos?" Have you ever asked the question, "Why is there life rather than deadness?" The answers to those questions have baffled scientists for the last few centuries, and the idea that nothing created everything is indeed being challenged, not just by people of faith, but by some scientists.

Since the dawn of civilization, man has gazed in awe at the stars, wondering what they are and how they got there. On a clear night, the unaided human eye can see about 6,000 stars. Prior to the 20th century, most scientists believed our own Milky Way galaxy was the entire universe, and that only about one hundred million stars existed. Then, in the early 20th century, astronomer Edwin Hubble discovered the universe is expanding. Rewinding the process mathematically, he calculated that everything in the universe, including matter, energy, space, and even time itself, had a beginning. Shockwaves rang loudly throughout the scientific community. Perhaps the most vocal adversary of a beginning to the universe was British astronomer Sir Fred Hoyle, who sarcastically said: "These theories were based on the hypothesis that all the matter in the universe was created in one big bang at a particular time in the remote past."[44] And now you know where the phrase, Big Bang Theory originated. But man-made satellites like the WMAP launched by NASA have mapped the differences in the temperature of the cosmic microwave background, the radiant heat remaining from the Big Bang across the sky and proven beyond any doubt that the universe had a one-time beginning in an incredible flash of light and energy.

During an interview with *Christianity Today* in 1982, Robert Jastrow, founder and for many years the director of the Goddard Institute for Space Studies admitted: "Astronomers now find they have painted themselves into a corner because they have proven, by their own methods, that the world began abruptly in an act of creation to which you can trace the seeds of every star, every planet, every living thing in this cosmos and on the earth. And they have found that all this happened as a product of forces they cannot hope to discover. That there are what I or anyone would call supernatural forces at work is now, I think, a scientifically proven fact."[45] Four years earlier, Jastrow wrote in his book *God and the Astronomers*: "For the scientist who has lived by his faith in the power of reason, the story ends like a bad dream. He has scaled the mountains of ignorance, he is about to conquer the highest peak; as he pulls himself over the final rock, he is greeted by a band of theologians who have been sitting there for centuries."[46] Physicists have determined that for life to exist, gravity and the other forces released at the moment our universe began had to be fine-tuned. Theoretical physicist Stephen Hawking, an agnostic, wrote: "The remarkable fact is that the values of these numbers seem to have been very finely adjusted to make possible the development of life."[47]

BIOLOGY - DNA IS CODED WITH INTELLIGENT INFORMATION

Astronomy is not the only area where science has seen evidence for design. Molecular biologists have discovered intricately complex designs in the microscopic world of DNA. In the past century, scientists learned that a tiny molecule called DNA is the "brains" behind each cell in our bodies as well as every other living thing. Yet the more they discover about DNA, the more amazed they are at the brilliance behind it. The coding behind DNA reveals such intelligence that it staggers the imagination. A mere pinhead of DNA contains information equivalent to a stack of paperback books that would encircle the earth 5,000 times. And DNA operates like a language with its own extremely complex software code. Microsoft founder Bill Gates says that the software of DNA is "far, far more complex than any software we have ever developed."

However, despite these stunning, revolutionary discoveries - the universe had a beginning - the universe is fine-tuned for life, and – DNA is coded with intelligent information, deception runs rampant. But, why, Denny? Great question. Let me try to explain.

CHARLES DARWIN

On December 27, 1831, at the age of twenty-two, a young British naturalist and geologist set out on a five-year-long voyage around the world on the HMS *Beagle*. His research established him as an eminent geologist whose observations and theories supported Charles Lyell's uniformitarian ideas, and publication of his journal of the voyage made him famous as a popular author.

DARWIN'S PUBLICATION

His research led him to publish in 1859, *On the Origin of Species by Means of Natural Selection*. Charles Darwin became internationally famous, and his pre-eminence as a scientist was honored by burial in Westminster Abbey. Darwin has been described as one of the most influential figures in human history.

DARWIN'S ADVOCATES

Sir Julian Huxley, grandson of Thomas Huxley, who coined the term *agnostic* and was the man most responsible for advancing Darwinism, said: "Darwin's theory is no longer a theory, but a fact ... Darwinianism has come of age so to speak. We are no longer having to bother about establishing the fact of evolution."[48] Isaac Asimov, a prolific American author and professor of biochemistry at Boston University said: "Today, although many educators play it safe by calling evolutionary ideas 'theory' instead of 'fact', there is no reputable biologist who doubts that species, including Homo sapiens, have developed with time, and that they are continually, though slowly, changing."[49] Oxford professor and author Richard Dawkins said: "It is absolutely safe to say that if you meet somebody who claims not to believe in evolution, that person is ignorant, or insane, (or wicked), but I'd rather not consider that."[50]

According to a book review written by Richard Fortey, published in *The Guardian:* "If Thomas Henry Huxley was famously 'Darwin's bulldog,' then Richard Dawkins is probably best described as 'Darwin's pit bull.'[51]" Dawkins wrote: "I am afraid I shall give God rather short shrift. He may have many virtues: no doubt he is invaluable as a pricker of the conscience and a comfort to the dying and the bereaved, but as an explanation of organized complexity he simply will not do. It is organized complexity we are trying to explain, so it is footling to invoke in explanation a being sufficiently organized and complex to create it." [52]

Professor Dawkins has targeted and mocked Christians throughout his career. And that is one of the reasons why Ben Stein challenged Richard Dawkins in an interview recorded for Mr. Stein's movie, *Expelled: No Intelligence Allowed.* Stein asked Dawkins about the origins of life on earth: "How did it get created?" Dawkins: "By a very slow process." Stein: "Well, how did it start?" Dawkins: "Nobody knows how it started. We know the kind of event that it must have been. We know the sort of event that must have happened for the origin of life." Stein: "And what was that?" Dawkins: "It was the origin of the first self-replicating molecule." Stein: "Right, and how did that happen?" Dawkins: "I told you; we don't know." Stein: "What do you think is the possibility that Intelligent Design might turn out to be the answer to some issues in genetics or in Darwinian evolution?" Dawkins: "Well, it could come about in the following way: It could be that at some earlier time, somewhere in the universe, a civilization evolved, probably by some kind of Darwinian means, probably to a very high level of technology, and designed a form of life they seeded onto perhaps this planet. Um, now that is a possibility, and an intriguing possibility. And I suppose it's possible that you might find evidence for that if you look at the details of biochemistry, molecular biology, you might find a signature of some sort of designer. And that designer could well be a higher intelligence from elsewhere in the universe. But that higher intelligence would itself have had to come about by some explicable, or ultimately explicable process. It couldn't have just jumped into existence spontaneously. That's the point."

In one of the most widely watched series in the history of Public Television, *Cosmos; A Personal Journey,* seen by over five hundred million people in sixty countries worldwide, host Carl Sagan stated the intended purpose for the project: "I believe our future depends powerfully on how we understand this cosmos. We wish to pursue the truth no matter where it leads. But to find the truth, we need imagination and skepticism both. We will not be afraid to speculate, but we will be careful to distinguish speculation from fact." Unfortunately, what Sagan stated in his series for television denies the very facts of the history of scientific research as it pertains to the theory of evolution.

In 1866, guided by the bias of evolution and atheism, German embryologist, and philosopher Ernst Haeckel, concluded that evolutionary stages of species from single cells to humans (phylogeny) were repeated in embryological development (ontogeny) of each species and drew a chart to demonstrate his hypothesis which became a standard used in biology in classrooms around the world. However, a comparison of Ernst Haeckel's drawings to actual photographs of the embryos he drew shows the speculative and deceptive nature of his "scientific" efforts.

The Miller–Urey experiment was an experiment that simulated hypothetical conditions thought at the time to be present on the early Earth and tested for the occurrence of chemical evolution. Specifically, the experiment tested Soviet scientist Alexander Oparin's and J. B. S. Haldane's hypothesis that conditions on the primitive Earth favored chemical reactions that synthesized organic compounds from inorganic precursors. Considered to be the classic experiment on the origin of life, it was conducted in 1952 and published in 1953 by Stanley Miller and Harold Urey at the University of Chicago. But what quantities of these acids were formed by spontaneous sparking? The amounts of detected amino acids were so miniscule that they were not reported using standard units of chemical concentration. In any origin of life by chance scenario, how did enough amino acids ever find one another amidst the sea of random chemicals? To assemble a car, all the required parts must be brought to the assembly line, not strewn all over the neighborhood. Similarly, no known natural mechanism gathers amino acids into proximity. Rather, nature tends to disperse such chemicals over time. Thus, according to the latest research, an intelligent agent was required to choose just the right set of building blocks for proteins. And a powerful agent was required to bring enough of those building blocks together into one place to form living cells. Random nature does not fit either description, but the God of the Bible does.

DARWIN'S CHALLENGERS

Thank God for scientists like Dr. Stephen C. Meyer who are confronting the theory of evolution by asking the question, "Where did the information that is required for constructing the diversity and complexity of life come from?" In his article, *Signature in the Cell*, Meyer wrote:

> When James Watson and Francis Crick elucidated the structure of DNA in 1953, they solved one mystery but created another. For almost one hundred years after the publication of Charles

Darwin's *The Origin of Species*, biology had rested secure in the knowledge that it had explained one of humankind's most enduring enigmas. From ancient times, observers had noticed organized structures in living organisms that gave the appearance of having been designed for a purpose—the elegant form and protective covering of the coiled nautilus, the interdependent parts of the eye, the interlocking bones, muscles, and feathers of a bird wing. But due in large measure to Watson and Crick's own discovery of the information-bearing properties of DNA, scientists have become increasingly, and in some quarters, acutely aware that there is at least one appearance of design in biology that has not been explained by natural selection or any other purely naturalistic mechanism. When Watson and Crick discovered the structure of DNA, they also discovered that DNA stores information in the form of a four-character alphabetic code. Strings of precisely sequenced chemicals called *nucleotide bases* store and transmit the assembly instructions — the information — for building the crucial protein molecules and protein machines the cell needs to survive. [53]

James Tour, Ph.D., is a synthetic organic chemist at Rice University. He has about 650 research publications and over two hundred patents. In 2015, he was inducted into the National Academy of Inventors. In 2013, he was named "Scientist of the Year" by *R&D Magazine*. In 2014, he was named among the fifty most influential scientists in the world, as well as "The World's Most Influential Scientific Minds." In August 2023, Dr. Tour issued a sixty-day public challenge to the ten top origin-of-life researchers, by name. He offered to take down all his public material, which exposed the fallacies of the origins-of-life explanations used by evolutionists, if they could answer just one of the five questions he posed to them. Not one of them presented a solution to any one of the problems listed in Dr. Tour's challenge, all of which must be resolved for the chemistry of life's origin to even be plausible through natural processes.[54]

Several years ago, I read Michael Behe's book, *Darwin's Black Box – The Biochemical Challenge to Evolution*. Here is a small portion of what I discovered. Within the cell there exist complex structures that bear similarity to an engine designed by humans - for instance, the flagellum that propels bacterium. All the necessary parts are there and function together as one system. So, how did evolution produce it one piece at a time? When viewed with an electron microscope, the individual parts resemble actual parts of a propulsion device with a stater, rotor, shaft, inner rings, outer rings, universal joint, and propeller. All of these are individual parts in a single-cell organism. The irreducible complexity may clearly be seen.

According to a review from the Discovery Institute:

> *Darwin's Black Box* thrust Michael Behe to the forefront of the intelligent design movement. The Lehigh University biochemist has haunted the dreams of Darwinists ever since. Each of his three books sparked a firestorm of criticism, in everything from the *New York Times* and the journal *Science* to the private blogs of professional atheists. Over the years, Behe has had a delightful time rebutting each attack, and now his responses are collected in a single volume entitled *A Mousetrap for Darwin*. The book's title alludes to Behe's homey illustration for his idea of irreducible complexity. A mousetrap with a missing part

doesn't work just a little worse. It doesn't work at all. The same goes for the bacterial flagellum pictured on the cover of the new collection. Ditto for an array of other ingenious molecular biological machines discovered in recent years. Can mindless evolutionary processes arrange biochemical parts into these complex functional wholes one small step at a time? Behe argues that a raft of new evidence — from the study of evolving microbes to the mutations in animals from dogs to polar bears — suggests that blind evolution cannot. [55]

In an article he wrote on the subject, David Lightsey pointed out that scientists like Jobe, Meyer, Tour, and Behe are not alone:

Information science, which is non-biological and therefore requires a programmer and not some theoretical step-by-step natural process, as well as all fields of biological sciences, clearly illustrate that the mind-boggling complexity of all living things, with all their interactive and interdependent functioning parts, are completely implausible to have occurred with any step-by-step process over eons of time. Time degrades things; it does not elevate them. This is one reason why more than 1,000 Ph.D. scientists from major universities such as Harvard, Princeton, Yale, MIT, UC Berkeley, Duke, John Hopkins, UCLA, Columbia, Rice, Stanford, etc. signed the *Scientific Dissent From Darwinism* statement, saying, "We are skeptical of the claims for the ability of random mutations and natural selection to account for the complexity of life. Careful examination of the evidence for Darwinian theory should be encouraged."[56]

Even so, the deception continues with prestigious magazines like *National Geographic* hedging the debate with sophisticated strategies of suppressing these newly discovered truths.

Against the black background of this never-ending suppression of the truth, there are those who speak out. Have you seen Focus On The Family's, *The Truth Project*? Released in 2006, this biblical worldview small group series has impacted over twenty million people in more than one hundred countries. In the introduction to lesson five, *Science: What is True?* the writer argues:

> Scientific investigation - "the systematic study of the structure and behavior of the physical and natural world through observation and experiment" – is also a valid way of ascertaining truth. Everywhere we look – whether up at the grandeur of the stars and galaxies or deep into the tiny and elegantly designed inner workings of a living cell – there is evidence that the cosmos is the handiwork of an intelligent, rational mind. In the contemplation of nature, we come face to face with the truth that God exists and that He has revealed Himself to us, not only through His written Word (special revelation) but also through the works of His hands (general revelation). Our natural reaction to this experience should be like that of a child: wonder, marvel, and praise for the Creator. The result is the propagation of a worldview that "scientifically" excludes the Creator, thus "freeing" mankind from accountability to a higher authority. The essence of Dr. Tackett's message may be summed up as follows: fallen man

ignores the plain evidence of objective scientific inquiry and promotes the atheistic philosophy of evolutionary theory primarily because he is determined to do as he pleases without answering to a higher authority.[57]

In the very first session in this twelve-part Christian worldview experience, Dr. Del Tackett asks his students an important question: "Why did Jesus come?" And although they offered many good answers, no one responded with the answer for which Dr. Tackett was looking. The answer that Dr. Tackett was looking for was what Jesus told Pontius Pilate: "For this cause I was born, and for this cause I have come into the world, that I should bear witness to the truth." [58] Jesus is the faithful witness to the truth in a sea of humanity that wants to suppress the truth and exchange the truth for the lie. And Jesus promised that His disciples would have access to the truth: "Then Jesus said to those Jews who believed Him, 'If you abide in My word, you are My disciples indeed. And you shall know the truth, and the truth shall make you free.'" [59] The freedom that the truth provides is what Jesus promised to any who would become His disciples. One of my favorite authors, Donald Grey Barnhouse, wrote: "Man's apostasy from God is not the act of an ignorant mind but the act of a determined will."[60]

In the most familiar passage in the New Testament, Jesus told Nicodemus:

> For God so loved the world that He gave His only begotten Son, that whoever believes in Him should not perish but have everlasting life. For God did not send His Son into the world to condemn the world, but that the world through Him might be saved. He who believes in Him is not condemned; but he who does not believe is

condemned already, because he has not believed in the name of the only begotten Son of God. And this is the condemnation, that the light has come into the world, and men loved darkness rather than light, because their deeds were evil. For everyone practicing evil hates the light and does not come to the light, lest his deeds should be exposed. [61]

You must write your own conclusion to this message. Either you now see yourself as a creature created by God, or you see yourself as a person who has been fooled by those who, although they profess to be wise, are fools and have suppressed the truth and/or exchanged the truth for the lie. But before you make up your mind, may I tell you what John the apostle wrote about Jesus Christ?

"He was in the world, and the world was made through Him, and the world did not know Him. He came to His own, and His own did not receive Him. But as many as received Him, to them He gave the right to become children of God, to those who believe in His name."[62]

THE THEORY OF EVOLUTION IS RACIST

Before we go any further, I must inform you that you may find the information I am about to share offensive. Please understand that to expose the facts, I may use some terms that may cause you to be offended, and if you are offended, please forgive me.

Darwin's publication is commonly known by only part of its' complete title: *On the Origin of Species by Means of Natural Selection*. However, the rest of Darwin's title is very revealing: *Or the Preservation of Favoured Races in the Struggle for Life*. His own writings confirm his perspective: "In Tierra del Sol I first saw bona fide savages, and they are as savage as the most curious person would desire – A wild man is indeed a miserable animal, but one worth seeing." [63] "At some future period, not very distant as measured by centuries, the civilized races of man will almost certainly exterminate and replace throughout the world the savage races."[64]

EUGENICS

In 1883, Sir Francis Galton – a cousin of Charles Darwin wrote in *Inquiries into Human Faculty and Its Development*: "We greatly want a brief word to express the science of improving stock … to give to the more suitable races or strains of blood a better chance of prevailing speedily over the less suitable than they otherwise would have had."[65] Galton is known as the father of Eugenics, a term which he coined and defined: "Eugenics is the study of the agencies under social control, that improve or impair the racial qualities of future generations either physically or mentally."[66] The rediscovery of Anglican Monk, Gregor Mendel's, laws of genetic inheritance in 1900 lent eugenics an air of scientific authority that would give the movement considerable force during the next three decades. Early posters used by this movement declared: "Eugenics is the self-direction of human evolution – Like a tree Eugenics draws its materials from many sources and organizes them into a harmonious entity." [67] The "harmonious entity" was the elimination of children with "less social and genetic worth," and the promotion of children with "more social and genetic worth." Nikola Tesla was a Serbian American inventor, electrical engineer, mechanical engineer, and futurist who predicted: "The year 2100 will see eugenics universally established. In past ages, the law governing the survival of the fittest roughly weeded out the less desirable strains. Then man's new sense of pity began to interfere with the ruthless workings of nature. As a result, we continue to keep alive and to breed the unfit."[68]

The eugenics movement in America received extensive funding from various corporate foundations including the Carnegie Institution, Rockefeller Foundation, and the Harriman railroad fortune, who financed a propaganda campaign that caught the attention of the American public with displays that loudly proclaimed: "Some people are born to be a burden on the rest – learn about heredity – you can help to correct these conditions." In 1906, John Henry Kellogg, the co-developer of Kellogg's Corn Flakes, provided funding to help found the Race Betterment Foundation in Battle Creek, Michigan. The foundation spent millions promoting Eugenics, including displays at the San Francisco Pan-American Expo in 1915, hiring and sending field worker to register human pedigrees and to promote their campaign *Fitter Families For Future Firesides*, which included contests which found families vying for medals. Eugenics was widely accepted in the U.S. academic community. By 1928 there were 376 separate university courses in some of the United States' leading schools, enrolling more than 20,000 students, which included eugenics in the curriculum.

The eugenic movement in Oregon was championed by a woman named Bethenia Angelina Owens-Adair, who was one of the first female physicians in Oregon. Her family traveled from her native Missouri to the Oregon Country via the Oregon Trail in 1843 with the Jesse Applegate wagon train. After years of her lobbying, in 1917 the Oregon State Legislature, in Salem, Oregon, passed a bill titled, *To Prevent Procreation of Certain Classes in Oregon*. Passage of the bill created the Oregon State Board of Eugenics, an organization that presided over the forced sterilization of more than 2,600 Oregon residents from 1917 to 1981. The United States was the first country to concertedly undertake compulsory sterilization programs for the purpose of eugenics. In the end, over 65,000 individuals were sterilized in thirty-three states under state compulsory sterilization programs in the United States.

Someone who ardently supported this national effort was Margaret Sanger, who wrote in - *A Plan for Peace*, published in 1932: "Apply a stern and rigid policy of sterilization and segregation to that grade of population whose progeny is already tainted or whose inheritance is such that objectionable traits may be transmitted to offspring."[69] In 1916, Margaret Sanger opened the first birth control clinic in the United States in New York's Brownsville neighborhood and was promptly arrested. In 1917, she started publishing the monthly periodical *Birth Control Review*. In 1921, Sanger founded the American Birth Control League, which later became the Planned Parenthood Federation of America. Since its' founding, that organization has championed abortion worldwide. The statistics are staggering: approximately seventy-three million per year, or 200,000 per day. And where they happen reveals the actual intent of that organization: eighty-three percent occur in developing countries while only thirteen percent occur in developed countries. Here in America, most Planned Parenthood abortion clinics are located in African American neighborhoods in inner cities.[70]

According to an article titled, *Secret Billionaire Club Seeks Population Control*, *The London Times* reported that some of the richest people in the world met secretly in New York to conspire on using their vast wealth to bring the world's population growth under control. The meeting included Bill Gates, David Rockefeller, Ted Turner, Oprah Winfrey, Warren Buffett, George Soros, and Michael Bloomberg. According to the *Times*, the billionaires were each given fifteen minutes to present their favorite cause. Over dinner they discussed how they might settle on an "umbrella cause" that would harness their interests. They agreed population control was the number one issue.[71]

Speaker of the House, Nancy Pelosi, proudly declared her position regarding using tax-payer money to fund abortions in America: "As a devout Catholic and mother of five in six years, I feel that God blessed my husband and me with our beautiful family," Pelosi said in the same breath as asserting that taxpayer-funded abortions are a "priority." "It's an issue of fairness and justice for *poorer women* in our country ... the right thing to do."[72] (emphasis mine) Pelosi draws attention to the underlying aim of abortion – it is directly aimed at the *poorer women*! But San Francisco Archbishop Salvatore Cordileone saw right through the sophistry. "To use the smokescreen of abortion as an issue of health and fairness to poor women is the epitome of hypocrisy: What about the health of the baby being killed?" he told *Catholic News Agency*. "What about giving poor women real choice, so they are supported in choosing life? The real 'devout Catholics' are the people of faith who run pro-life crisis pregnancy clinics; they are the only ones who provide poor women life-giving alternatives to having their babies killed in their wombs."[73]

Due to their exhaustive research, Robert G. Marshall and Charles A. Donovan exposed the racial prejudice and avarice that birthed the abortion industry in America: "Among the many insidious initiatives associated with Sanger was The Negro Project. Conceived by Dr. Clarence Gamble, the main idea was to recruit charismatic black ministers who would encourage black women to practice birth control, thereby reducing the number of black babies being born."[74] According to manuscripts in the Sophia Smith Collection kept at Smith College in North Hampton, Massachusetts, Margaret Sanger wrote to suggest their "Negro Project" should train ordained ministers to champion their efforts. The letter dated December 10, 1939, was addressed to Clarence J. Gamble, M.D.: "The minister's work is also important, and also he should be trained, perhaps by the Federation as to our ideals and the goals we hope to reach. We don't want the word to go out that we want to exterminate the Negro population, and the minister is the man who can straighten out that idea if it ever occurs to any of their more rebellious members." Anyone familiar with Darwin's writings can make the connection.

One of Charles Darwin's disciples, Sir Thomas Huxley, wrote

in *Lay Sermons, Addresses and Reviews* 1871: "No rational man, cognizant of the facts, believes that the average Negro is the equal, still less the superior, of the white man … It is simply incredible to think that … he will be able to compete successfully with his bigger-brained and smaller-jawed rival."[75] A well-respected scientist and evolutionist who made the cover of *TIME* magazine, Henry F. Osborn, Director of the American Museum of Natural History, wrote an article titled *The Evolution of Human Races*, which was published by *Natural History* magazine in 1926. Here is an excerpt: "The Negroid stock is even more ancient than the Caucasian and the Mongolian, as may be proved by an examination not only of the brain, of the hair, of the bodily characters, such as the teeth, the genitalia, the sense organs, but of the instincts, the intelligence. The standard of intelligence of the average adult Negro is similar to that of the eleven-year-old youth of the species *Homo sapiens*."[76]

THE HOLOCAUST

Scottish anthropologist, Sir Arthur Keith, an evolutionist, and anti-Semite wrote *Evolution and Ethics* in 1947, and in his article stated: "The German Fuhrer, as I have consistently maintained, is an evolutionist; he has consistently sought to make the practices of Germany conform to the theory of evolution."[77] Indeed, Adolf Hitler was a devote evolutionist who wrote in *Mein Kampf*: "As its bearers and representatives, the leadership principle must have a body of men who have passed through a process of selection lasting over several years, who have been tempered by the hard realities of life and thus rendered capable of carrying the principle into practical effect." So, Hitler selected a group of men who over time would carry out his "principles."

The Olympic Games were awarded to Berlin in 1931, two years before the Nazis came to power in Germany. Hitler saw the

Games as an opportunity to promote his government and ideals of racial supremacy, and the official Nazi party paper wrote in the strongest terms that Jews and Black people should not be allowed to participate in the Games. However, when threatened with a boycott of the Games by other nations, he relented and allowed Black people and Jews to participate. African American track star Jesse Owens won four gold medals in the sprints and long jump events. The photo of Owens saluting during the playing of our National Anthem while his German competitor Luz Long gave the Nazi salute is a classic symbol of the growing conflict that led to World War II.

According to a book written by James M. Rhodes, Hitler prioritized his hatred of what he called the inferior races and maintained a Hit List.[78]

<u>Hitler's Hit List</u>

- <u>Nordic</u> – close to pure Aryan
- <u>Germanic</u> – predominately Aryan
- <u>Mediterranean</u> – slightly Aryan
- <u>Slavic</u> – close to half-Aryan, half Ape
- <u>Oriental</u> – slight Ape preponderance
- <u>Black African</u> – predominantly Ape
- <u>Jewish</u> – close to pure Ape

In stark contrast to Hitler's hatred, Christian children all over the world sing, "Red and Yellow, Black, and White, they are precious in his sight. Jesus loves the little children of the world."

Hitler and his henchmen ultimately arrived at what has been called, "The Final Solution to the Jewish Question" – the extermination of the Jewish race in Europe. Let history note that indeed Hitler and his henchmen implemented that plan that murdered six million men women and children in Nazi concentration camps, but the seeds were sown by Charles

Darwin's writing, *On the Origin of Species by Natural Selection or the Preservation of Favoured Races in the Struggle for Life*.

On April 12, 1945, General Dwight D. Eisenhower arrived at the Nazi Concentration Camp at Orhdruf, Germany, accompanied by General Omar Bradley, General George Patton, and others. He was so appalled by what he saw and what he heard from survivors who had been liberated just eight days previously, he cabled President Harry S. Truman to ask him to send a delegation of U.S. Government officials and journalist to ensure that the world would never be able to deny the atrocities he had just witnessed firsthand. News repoprters and photograpjers arrived and witnessed firsthand and reported what they saw: "American troops, including African American soldiers from the Headquarters and Service Company of the 183rd Engineer Combat Battalion, 8th Corps, U.S. 3rd Army, view corpses stacked behind the crematorium during an inspection tour of the Buchenwald concentration camp. Buchenwald, Germany, April 17, 1945."

Those who champion Critical Race Theory ought to be reminded about the irreversible damage done by the deception developed by Darwin and his disciples throughout the last 160+ years of human history.

THE THEORY OF EVOLUTION IS SEXIST

Evolution is not only racist, but also sexist. In 1871, Charles Darwin wrote in *Descent of Man and Selection in Relation to Sex*: "The chief distinction in the intellectual powers of the two sexes is shown by man's attaining to a higher eminence, in whatever he takes up, than can woman, whether requiring deep thought, reason, or imagination, or merely the use of the senses and hands, men are capable of a decided pre-eminence over women in many subjects, the average of mental power in man must be above that of woman."[79] Sigmund Freud was a student and follower of

Charles Darwin and drew his conclusions accordingly: "Mental disorders are the vestiges of behavior that had been appropriate in earlier stages of evolution."[80]

THE SEXUAL REVOLUTION

The embracing of the theory of evolution spawned the sexual revolution. When noted evolutionist Sir Julian Huxley was asked why people so quickly embraced the theory of evolution, he replied, "It is because the concept of a Creator-God interferes with our sexual mores. Thus, we have rationalized God out of existence."[81] The sexual revolution of the 60's and 70's led to a further degradation of human sexuality foreseen in the Bible. As Paul the apostle wrote: "For this reason God gave them up to vile passions. For even their women exchanged the natural use for what is against nature. Likewise also the men, leaving the natural use of the woman, burned in their lust for one another, men with men committing what is shameful, and receiving in themselves the penalty of their error which was due."[82]

Anyone who honestly reads the Bible and takes it literally must conclude that the suppression of the truth and exchanging the truth of God for the lie has dire consequences for any individual, community, or nation. The downward spiral manifests itself in homosexuality and other perversions of God's design for humanity, but that is the end of the road, not the beginning. Today, Christians are called "homophobic" and "hate mongers" by a society that can only blame itself for the current conditions in which it finds itself. The Bible identifies how a nation enters the vortex of disintegration of morality. The Lord revealed to His prophet, Ezekiel, the underlying cause of the wickedness of Sodom: "Look, this was the iniquity of your sister Sodom: She and her daughter had pride, fullness of food, and abundance of idleness; neither did she strengthen the hand of the poor and needy." [83] The underlying cause of Sodom's wickedness were her citizen's pride, prosperity, and pursuit of pleasure which produced apathy and complacency toward the less fortunate. Then the Lord revealed the result: "And they were haughty and committed abomination before Me; therefore, I took them away as I saw *fit.*"[84]

Let's dig deeper and consider God's perspective and dealings with the cities of Sodom & Gomorrah. Before I begin, please let me assure you that I want to convey information, not condemnation.

The summer between my Sophomore and Junior years at E.W. Clark High School in Las Vegas, Nevada, was one of the best summers I have ever experienced. My childhood friend, Terry, and I were born one month apart in 1950. Our families were next door neighbors on 8th Street in Livermore, California at the time we were both born. Terry was always climbing, and I was always scootin' or bikin.' We were both men on the move. We were best buddies, and we shared everything, even helping ourselves to my birthday cake when I turned three. Even after my family moved to a new home, we were together all the time. Our mothers were best friends, too. My dad was a journalist, and Terry's dad was the swimming coach at Livermore High School. Terry and I stayed in touch throughout our childhood although both our parents got divorced while we were young. Terry's mother got remarried and moved to Duarte in Southern California and I moved to Las Vegas with my mother, stepfather, and two older brothers, and when Terry moved to his bachelor father's home in Glendora, we planned a month-long summer vacation together. In the summer of 1966, our plans were rewarded as Terry, his dad and I traveled together in their VW beetle from Southern California across the Columbia River by ferry and all the way to the tip of the Olympic Peninsula in Washington and back, hiking, camping, fishing, and climbing all along the way. After our exciting adventures together were concluded, we made immediate plans to do it again the very next summer.

As fantastic as that experience had been, the following

summer was the exact opposite; one of the most difficult and disappointing times I have ever experienced in my life. Shortly after I finished my Junior year in High School, two good friends of mine and I were injured in a single-car accident. Trying to get home in a hurry from an afternoon of hunting jack rabbits in the desert near Red Rock Canyon, we sped down Charleston Boulevard at 70 mph, hit a dip in the road, flew forty-six feet through the air, and rolled Craig's Triumph convertible sportscar three times before coming to a stop 469 feet down the road. Not wearing seat belts, we were all thrown from the car as it rolled. After several days in the hospital, I was totally bummed out. Now our plans to revisit our terrific time together the summer before were shelved. Terry got a summer job, and I just tried to recover from my injuries before my Senior year started in September. Then Terry's dad called to say that he would be happy to take me along on a pared-down version of last summer's trek together. Because of my head injuries, the doctors approved the trip if we did not get above 6,000 feet elevation. Although weakened by the accident, I was excited about the kind offer, and looked forward to our time camping, hiking, and fishing together even without my best friend, Terry, along for the adventure.

I was not prepared for what I was about to encounter. My expectations would be destroyed by what loomed ahead of me. The first few days of our journey were okay. Then I was shocked by Terry's dad's physical advances. It started out as backrubs that he gave me while I lay in my sleeping bag in our tent after a long day of travel. It became excruciatingly uncomfortable as I began to realize that he wanted something much more. As we were riding together in his VW beetle a few days into our journey, he reached over and touched my leg in a way that repulsed me instantly and caused me to respond by demanding that he take me immediately to my grandparents' home, fortunately not far away in Calistoga, California. He protested, but I was persistent. When we arrived there, I unpacked my belongings and said goodbye to a man I had deeply loved and trusted all my life. It was the last time I saw him or had any contact with him. After he left, I told my godly grandparents what had happened, called my mother in Las Vegas, and spent the next few days at the horse ranch where my grandparents lived and worked, waiting for my mom to drive up and get me, and recoiling from the shocking and terribly disappointing discovery I had encountered about Terry's dad. All the way on that long drive back home, my mother and I tried to cope with our feelings. We had a tough time understanding what had happened.

Since that day so long ago, I have known personally and as a pastor many men and women who have made the decision to give in to unnatural sexual desires. I have witnessed the devastation that both heterosexual and homosexual sin has created in the lives of people for whom I deeply care. Our family watched in helpless agony as my wife's homosexual younger brother contracted HIV and we watched him waste away and die of AIDS in 1990. I have great compassion for those whose lives are being destroyed, not only physically, but spiritually and emotionally by homosexuality. But I also recognize and absolutely believe what the Bible has to say about homosexuality. It is sin, just as certainly as adultery is sin. It is not a sickness, it is sin. No one has an excuse for the personal choices for which God holds us responsible. God's word reveals that homosexuality is the result of personal choices an individual makes when God has been rejected and replaced by that individual. I have also witnessed firsthand the transforming power of the Holy Spirit within a sinner's life who have repented of their sinful choices and received the forgiveness that Jesus Christ offers to any and all who come to Him. I have seen adulterers and homosexuals; alcoholics and drug addicts; delivered from their former lifestyle and watched them discover freedom from guilt and shame and the joy of living according to God's design for them. Sadly, tragically, governments have banned what they describe as "conversion therapy" and threatened Christian counselors with fines and/or imprisonment for their efforts to rescue people trapped in bondage to sin.

HOMOSEXUAL ACTIVISM

Although I have compassion for the individual who chooses a homosexual life, I am not ignorant of the fact that there exists a homosexual activist agenda that threatens not only the individual but threatens our society and everyone in it. Jesus said that rampant sexual immorality would be a sign that would precede His Second Coming. On June 19, 1969, the homosexual political movement in America, which had previously defined its goal as "the right to be left alone," took a militant turn when New York Police tried to arrest an underage homosexual patron at the Stonewall Inn in Greenwich Village. As a result, LGBTQ activists rioted with the police. That episode of violent rebellion is now commemorated annually as Pride Day. Cities across America host Pride parades on June 19th featuring floats sponsored by some of the largest corporations in America. The Stonewall Inn is the site that President Obama selected for the first-ever national monument commemorating the battle for LGBTQ rights, reportedly because it is "The birthplace of America's modern LGBTQ liberation movement."

In his *An Open Letter to Christian Leaders in America*, Pastor Scott Lively warned:

> The inspiration for the rioters was Herbert Marcuse, the German-born philosopher and political strategist who headed the "Frankfort School" of Cultural Marxism. From a perch in the highest branches of American academia Marcuse railed against "the repressive order of procreative sexuality" and called for the "disintegration of

the … monogamic and patriarchal family." In 1972, two hundred homosexual organizations, representing the entire LGBT movement, met in Chicago to outline their Marcusian agenda: a blueprint for supplanting Biblical morality with sexual anarchy — in essence, the overthrow of family-centered Christian civilization. In 1973, their "long march through the institutions" began with the political takeover of the American Psychiatric Association to redefine homosexuality as psychologically healthy. Just forty years later, in 2013, the last secular institution to resist LGBT bullying was finally subdued - the Boy Scouts of America. One last barrier to LGBTQ cultural hegemony remains: the Christian church. All the battle-hardened "LGBTQ rights" activists with all of their formidable resources are mobilized for an assault on Christianity itself under the hijacked rainbow banner of "LGBTQ Theology." Indeed, the process has already begun, like the retreat of the tide before the tsunami.[85]

MISPLACED BLAME

Warning – this is not Christianity Lite. This will be no sermonette for Christianettes. I will not sound tolerant or be politically correct. But I will speak with personal conviction and compassion. It is not my aim to offend anyone or alienate anyone. However, it is my aim to speak frankly and without compromise about a subject that is extremely controversial and contentious.

Some people who call themselves Christians place blame for the problems we face on our current President and his administration. Others place blame on our elected leaders in Congress. Some people who call themselves Christians blame the legalization of marijuana and other drugs for our current problems. No one can estimate the damage done by our drug culture even as heroin becomes the drug of choice and methamphetamine addiction continues to wreak havoc on users and death by fentanyl becomes the leading cause of death among our younger population. Some people who call themselves Christians in this country believe that judgment is coming because of the growth and public flaunting of homosexuality in America even while many men who call themselves Christians contribute to the multi-billion dollar per year pornography business in America. Some blame the abortion industry in this nation led by Planned Parenthood and its' founder, Margaret Sanger, who spread the propaganda of Eugenics and spawned an abortion industry which has murdered over sixty million unborn babies since the US Supreme Court ruled that abortion was a woman's legal right. However, all these current problems are not the reason God will judge America. These current problems are part of the judgment that God promised would come upon His people if THEY chose to disobey and forsake Him. These are symptoms of judgment, not the cause of judgment. You will be shocked to know that God holds His people responsible for these current conditions. If we were obedient to Him – we would be the salt and light that preserves and illuminates in these corrupt dark days!

Peter the apostle wrote about the judgment of God: "For the time *has come* for judgment to begin at the house of God; and if *it begins* with us first, what will *be* the end of those who do not obey the gospel of God?"[86] So, Denny, what and where is the house of God? Great question – the Bible has the answer. Paul the apostle clearly identified the house of God when he wrote to Timothy: "*I write* so that you may know how you ought to conduct yourself in the house of God, which is the church of the living God, the pillar and ground of the truth."[87] So, Peter wrote that judgment would begin at church. Why, you ask? One of the sad realities in

Bible prophecy as it relates to the end of the age is the stated fact that instead of the church becoming better as the age progresses, it will grow worse and end in utter apostasy.

FAILED LEADERSHIP

The blame for that ultimate result lies certainly on the shoulders of the leaders within the church. A survey of one thousand Christian pastors across seven major denominations in the United States conducted by George Barna, director of research with the Cultural Research Center at Arizona Christian University and senior fellow at the Center for Biblical Worldview with the Family Research Council revealed that only thirty-seven percent of clergy in America hold a Biblical worldview. Barna analyzed the answers provided by the pastors to questions regarding fifty-four beliefs and behaviors, including salvation through Jesus Christ alone, absolute Biblical and moral truth, human purpose, sanctity of human life and other Biblical doctrines.

In commenting on the study, Barna offered these three observations: "First, the old labels attached to families of churches are not as useful as they were in the past," Barna noted. "The best example is the term 'evangelical,' which has traditionally connoted churches where the Bible is revered and is taught as God's reliable and relevant word for our lives. With barely half of evangelical pastors possessing a biblical worldview—and that number continuing to decline—attending what may be considered an 'evangelical' church no longer ensures a pastoral staff that has a high view of the scriptures."[88]

Barna also touched on a centuries-old division. "The theological rift between Protestant and Catholic churches remains intact, though neither segment is doing a proficient job of making the Bible a trustworthy and authoritative guide for people's life." He continued, "While the forty percent of all Protestant pastors holding a biblical worldview far exceeds the six percent among Roman Catholic priests, both of those incidence levels are disturbingly low. Our study among the public in 2021 revealed that only five percent of adults who regularly attend a Protestant church, and just one percent of those regularly attending Catholic churches, have a biblical worldview, so neither segment of churches is getting the job done."[89] In 2023, during a presentation at Family Research Council's *Pray, Vote and Stand Summit*, Barna explained:

"That's barely one of every three who buy into God's Word to such an extent that their life is driven by Biblical truth. It's appalling. Think about that for a moment. What does evangelical even mean if the pastor doesn't buy into the Scriptures and teach those things to his people?"[90] Barna went on to say that fifty-one percent of lay people surveyed claim to have a Biblical worldview, but when their beliefs and behaviors are measured by what he described as the seven cornerstones of a Biblical worldview only six percent of American adults see the world through the lens of Scripture.[91]

Barna's seven cornerstones of a Biblical worldview are:

- God is the eternal, omniscient, omnipotent, and just Creator.
- Humans are sinful by nature.
- Jesus Christ grants forgiveness of sin and eternal life when sinners repent and profess their faith in Him alone.
- The Bible is true, reliable, and always relevant.
- Absolute moral truth exists.
- Success is defined as consistent obedience to God.
- Life's purpose is to know, love and serve God with all one's heart, mind, strength, and soul.

Barna cited the correlation between a pastor's failure to practice personal spiritual disciplines and their abandonment of the truths found in the Bible: "While studying the spiritual behavioral patterns of pastors it became evident that a large share of them does not have a regular spiritual routine. There was a correlation between possessing Biblical beliefs and a consistent regimen of Bible reading, prayer, worship and confession, and one-third of all pastors do not read the Bible during a typical week." Barna likened such a dereliction of duty to surgeons not washing their hands before surgery. "It's unthinkable, almost unimaginable," he said. "Given that Bible reading is a major source of spiritual nourishment, no wonder so many pastors are spiritually weak and ineffective. Add to that their frequent failure to pray, to connect with God through worship and thanksgiving, to spend time seeking God's direction and will, or regularly returning to Him to confess their sins and ask for forgiveness—it's no wonder so many pastors struggle." Barna described the sad result of that dereliction of duty: "Because pastors teach what they believe, many churches are becoming centers of syncretism and secular thought. Thousands of pastors have become leaders of a movement away from God, toward narcissism."[92]

Barna's research and analysis remind me of God's indictment of the corrupt spiritual leaders in Israel when He said to His prophet, Ezekiel:

> Woe to the shepherds of Israel who feed themselves! Should not the shepherds feed the flocks? You eat the fat and clothe yourselves with the wool; you slaughter the fatlings, *but* you do not feed the flock. The weak you have not strengthened, nor have you healed those who were sick, nor bound up the broken, nor brought back what was driven away, nor sought what was lost; but with force and cruelty you have ruled them. So they were scattered because *there was* no shepherd; and they became food for all the beasts of the field when they were scattered. My

sheep wandered through all the mountains, and on every high hill; yes, My flock was scattered over the whole face of the earth, and no one was seeking or searching *for them.*[93]

God sent a warning to His prophet Jeremiah that pastors would be wise to heed: "'Woe to the shepherds who destroy and scatter the sheep of My pasture!' says the LORD. Therefore thus says the LORD God of Israel against the shepherds who feed My people: 'You have scattered My flock, driven them away, and not attended to them. Behold, I will attend to you for the evil of your doings,' says the LORD."[94] The apostle Paul warned the elders of Ephesus: "Therefore take heed to yourselves and to all the flock, among which the Holy Spirit has made you overseers, to shepherd the church of God which He purchased with His own blood. For I know this, that after my departure savage wolves will come in among you, not sparing the flock. Also from among yourselves men will rise up, speaking perverse things, to draw away the disciples after themselves."[95] The apostle Paul warned Timothy: "For the time will come when they will not endure sound doctrine, but according to their own desires, *because* they have itching ears, they will heap up for themselves teachers; and they will turn *their* ears away from the truth, and be turned aside to fables."[96]

JUDGMENT

In 1980, scientists were drawn to beautiful Mount Saint Helens in Southern Washington because of a series of earthquakes and the visible bulging of the northern flank of the mountain. In addition to the seismic activity, the dormant volcano began to intermittently vent steam into the air. As the intensity and frequency of these events grew, authorities warned residents to evacuate the area. But there was one resident, Harry Randall Truman, the owner, and operator of Spirit Lake Lodge who refused to heed the warnings as he stated: "I don't have any idea whether it will blow, but I don't believe it to the point that I'm going to pack up." Harry became somewhat of a celebrity as his stubborn refusal to evacuate became local, then national news. He stated his reasons clearly: "If the mountain goes, I'm going with it. This area is heavily timbered, Spirit Lake is in between me and the mountain, and the mountain is a mile away, the mountain ain't gonna hurt me, boy." Then, on a beautiful sunny Sunday morning – May 18, 1980 – at 8:32am, a 5.1 earthquake shook loose the bulging north flank, resulting in the largest known landslide in history as removal of more than half a cubic mile of material released pressure and triggered a devastating lateral blast and ash-laden eruptive column. The lateral blast outran the landslide – initially moving at 220 miles per hour but quickly accelerating to 670 mph; overtaking cars frantically trying to flee like the one driven by photographer Reid Blackburn.

In a matter of moments, 230 square miles of old-growth forests were blown down – leveled as if some giant comb had been run through them - blowing away every branch and needle and laying them down in the same direction of the super-heated pyroclastic flows. An eruption column rose 80,000 feet (15 mi) into the atmosphere and deposited ash in eleven U.S. states. At the same time, snow, ice, and several entire glaciers on the volcano melted, forming a series of large lahars (volcanic mudslides) that reached as far as the Columbia River, fifty miles to the southwest. The event was the deadliest and most economically destructive volcanic eruption in the history of the United States. Fifty-seven people were killed and two hundred houses, twenty-seven bridges, fifteen miles of railways and 185 miles of highway were destroyed. After the smoke and ash had cleared, the area of complete devastation was seen dramatically as a scar upon the landscape by astronauts orbiting earth. Side-by-side photos published by news media provided a vivid comparison to the before and after of poor old Harry Randall Truman and the Spirit Lake Lodge, his dog, and his sixteen cats who refused to heed the warnings and evacuate while they could.

Of course, Harry was an adult and made his own choice about how he perceived the data being collected and reported by experts trained to recognize the danger of Harry's proximity to Mount Saint Helens. Sadly, even some of those experts perished in the violent eruption. Each of us is responsible for surveying the threat of danger and making choices that protect us from that danger. Sure, we all take risks every day, but it is incumbent on each of us to be vigilant and careful. And we need to protect those who are not aware of impending danger by giving them accurate information so that they may decide for themselves how to deal with the danger.

My wife, Vickie, and I have ten hens in a coop and a hen house in our backyard. We love fresh eggs, and they provide us with that as we feed and care for them. It was on a late afternoon while our hens were free ranging out of the protection of their home, roaming freely, and pecking and scratching all around our yard that Vickie heard the unmistakable screech of a hawk. Looking up, we could see the predator soaring at tree-top level and occasionally darting and diving among the tall fir trees that surround our home. Unaware of the danger this invader posed to them, the hens were difficult to round up and herd back into the safety of their coop. How do you convey to a chicken that their very existence was in peril, and if they did not run to safety, they could have been a hawk's meal? Thankfully, we were able to lure them in with some fresh greens from Vickie's raised bed garden. The hawk flew off to seek its' dinner elsewhere and the danger was past.

Thanks for the history, and the chicken chatter, Denny – but what is the point? Great question. In Peter's second letter, he pointed out that God's righteous judgment in the past has been cosmic, global, and local – those are the facts. And yet, since amid those judgments God delivered Noah and Lot, then God knows how to deliver the godly when His judgment will once again be global and universal. Even as God delivers the godly, those already judged by God will be kept, held, reserved for their final judgment:

> For if God did not spare the angels who sinned, but cast *them* down to hell and delivered *them* into chains of darkness, to be reserved for judgment; and did not spare the ancient world, but saved Noah, *one of* eight *people,* a preacher of righteousness, bringing in the flood on the world of the ungodly; and turning the cities of Sodom and Gomorrah into ashes, condemned *them* to destruction, making *them* an example to those who afterward would live ungodly; and delivered righteous Lot, *who was* oppressed by the filthy conduct of the wicked (for that righteous man, dwelling among them, tormented *his* righteous soul from day to day by seeing and hearing *their* lawless deeds) - then the Lord knows how to deliver the godly out of temptations and to reserve the unjust under punishment for the day of judgment. [97]

Peter investigated the past and stated that God's judgment has been COSMIC. Peter identified them for us – "the angels who sinned." Peter investigated the past and stated that God's judgment has not only been cosmic but has also been GLOBAL. Peter identified this judgment for us – "the ancient world." Peter investigated the past and stated that God's judgment has not only been cosmic and global but has also been LOCAL. Peter identified this judgment for us – "the cities of Sodom and Gomorrah." Please understand that the judgment and destruction that happened to these individuals is not the end of them. No, they are now reserved for judgment. They are "the angels who sinned," "the ancient world," and "the cities of Sodom and Gomorrah."

Although God's judgment on a sinful creation is inevitable, it is not inescapable - Peter told us of two exceptions who were rescued from judgment. "Noah, one of eight people," and "righteous Lot." So, question – are you reserved for judgment or are you rescued from judgment? The choice is yours. Before you answer that question, please remember what Harry Randall Truman said: "I don't have any idea whether it will blow. But I don't believe it to the point that I'm going to pack up. If the mountain goes, I'm going with it. This area is heavily timbered, Spirit Lake is in between me and the mountain, and the mountain is a mile away, the mountain ain't gonna hurt me, boy."

The apostle Paul revealed this impending global, universal day of judgment when he addressed the Greek philosophers at Mars Hill in Athens 1,900 years ago: "Because He has appointed a day on which He will judge the world in righteousness by the Man whom He has ordained. He has given assurance of this to all by raising Him from the dead."[98] Now, it is easy to conger up a picture of an angry, mean-spirited judge. But please reject that picture and understand that Paul identified the One who is coming to judge the world in righteousness is Jesus Christ, the One who laid down His life on the Cross because of His great love!

CHAPTER 3

DECEPTION AS A SOCIAL / ECONOMIC PHENOMENON

So FAR, WE HAVE INVESTIGATED deception as an intellectual / scientific phenomenon. Now, let's investigate deception as a social / economic phenomenon.

Have you seen the documentary *An Inconvenient Truth, A Global Warning*? Former Vice-President Al Gore has flown in his private jet all over the planet preaching the evils of "Climate Change." The 2007 Nobel Peace Prize was shared, in two equal parts, between the Intergovernmental Panel on Climate Change (IPCC) and Al Gore, and the citation issued along with the prize by the award committee indicated their enthusiasm for the direction their efforts were headed: "For their efforts to build up and disseminate greater knowledge about man-made climate change, and to lay the foundations for the measures that are needed to counteract such change" Have you ever asked yourself, "Where did he get his passion for this issue?" In 1992, while serving as a US Senator, Al Gore published a book, *Earth in the Balance: Ecology and the Human Spirit*. Al Gore's website provides a clue to his passion: *"Earth In The Balance* helped place the environment on the national agenda; now, as environmental issues move front-and-center in the public consciousness, the time is right to reflect deeply on the fate of our planet and commit ourselves to its future."

So, it is "the fate of our planet" that motivates Mr. Gore's efforts. On page 260 of his book, Mr. Gore cites with approval the statement that "the prevailing ideology of belief in prehistoric Europe and much of the world was based on the worship of a single earth goddess,"[99] and then he goes on to lament that "organized goddess worship was eliminated by Christianity."[100] What Mr. Gore was alluding to is the fact that long before Darwin put forth his theory of evolution, the pagan world had believed that the universe is eternal and that its development was and is guided by what today would be named Mother Earth or Mother Nature. The Bible clearly teaches that the earth is not our mother; it is the theater upon which the Creator has placed humanity to steward. Paganism, however, considers the earth itself to be the creator of all living things, evolving itself while controlling the geological processes and the biological evolution of its plants and animals.

But this is not just an ancient belief, it is a current trend among many intelligent scientists like James Lovelock, who wrote: "The evolution of the species and the evolution of their environment are tightly coupled together as a single and inseparable process."[101] In an article he wrote about Lovelock's work, published in the prestigious *Scientific American*, Tim Beardsley stated: "Lovelock's musings have had two consequences. They inspired a quasi-political movement based in London, complete with a publishing arm, that now includes thousands of adherents throughout the U.S. and Western Europe. Indeed, Gaia has almost become the official ideology of "Green" parties in Europe: it appeals naturally to scientifically innocent individuals who worry about the environment."[102] Another distinguished scientist, Rupert Sheldrake with a Ph.D. from Cambridge University wrote: "But today, with the rise of the green movement, Mother Nature is reasserting herself, whether we like it or not. In particular, the acknowledgement that our planet is a living organism, Gaia,

Mother Earth, strikes a responsive chord in millions of people."[103] Indeed, it is not only millions of people around the world who have embraced the Green Movement, but that deceptive idea has been at the center of environmental activism in politics, locally, nationally, and globally.

Carl Sagan endorsed Al Gore's book when he wrote: "A global environmental crisis threatens to overwhelm our children's generation. Mitigating the crisis will require a planetary perspective, long-term thinking, political courage and savvy, eloquence, and leadership—all of which are in evidence in Al Gore's landmark book." The sentiments expressed in Sagan's endorsement are in lockstep with what Sir Julian Huxley, first director-general of UNESCO (United Nations Educational, Scientific and Cultural Organization), wrote: "Thus the general philosophy of UNESCO should, it seems, be a scientific world humanism, global in extent and evolutionary in background. The unifying of traditions into a single common pool of experience, awareness and purpose is the necessary prerequisite for further major progress in human evolution. Accordingly, although political unification in some sort of world government will be required for the definitive attainment of this state, unification in the things of the mind is not only necessary also, but it can pave the way for other types of unification."[104]

AGENDA 21

Allow me to introduce you to Agenda 21, an action plan of the United Nations related to sustainable development that was an outcome of the United Nations Conference on Environment and Development (UNCED) held in Rio de Janeiro, Brazil, in 1992. Unanimously agreed upon by the nations represented there, including the United States, it outlines four sections: 1 - Social and Economic Dimensions, 2 - Conservation and Management of Resources for Development, 3 - Strengthening the Role of Major Groups, and 4 - Means of Implementation. In addition to its four sections, it presented three circles of change – economic development, social progress, and environmental responsibility that would intersect and create a fair world, a livable world, and a viable world with the prospects for sustainable development. The first of these three circles of change is Equity – or social justice explained as "Our God-given unalienable rights must be set aside for the common good of the collective." The second circle of change is Economy and was explained as the redistribution of wealth among nations and the replacement of "free enterprise" with "free trade" creating government affiliated businesses and business interests. And the third circle of change is Environment and was explained as the abolishment of private property, property rights and the management of natural resources for the saving of the world.

EQUITY

Equity first targets our children via books, the internet, and other social media and includes the revamping of our colleges and universities. Dr. Chester M. Pierce, Professor of Education at Harvard, addressing the Association for Childhood Education International in April 1972 said, "Every child in America entering school at the age of five is mentally ill, because he comes to school with certain allegiances to our founding fathers, toward our elected officials, toward his parents, toward a belief in a supernatural being, and toward the sovereignty of this nation as a separate entity. It is up to you as teachers to make all of these sick children well by creating the international child of the future. "[105]

Tony Perkins, President of Family Research Council, wrote in a letter dated August 13, 2014:

In just a few short weeks, millions of American students will head back to school. You should be very concerned about the spreading, hidden nightmare facing them in school today: public schools, private, religious, even home schools. I'm not talking about bullies, playground predators, or school violence. I'm referring to the morally corrupt federal takeover of education called Common Core -- or as I prefer to call it – OBAMACORE. If Obamacore is allowed to take control of America's educational system, I foresee a nation where children are indoctrinated with a liberal ideology that celebrates sexual perversion, worships the creation rather than the Creator, all at the expense of academic achievement and our nation's Christian heritage. All indications are that the standards imposed by Obamacore will actually hamper education rather than improve it. Obamacore opens education to even more propaganda in class than we are experiencing today. Its "one-size-fits-all" approach not only eliminates more advanced material, but also makes it difficult for teachers to teach students individually. Typical of other liberal programs, rather than raise up underperformers, Obamacore will lower standards of higher-performing states in order to 'level the playing field.'

Sadly, many of our leaders just don't get it. Former Florida Gov. Jeb Bush (founder of the Foundation for Excellence in Education) is a proponent of Common Core. Bush called Common Core a strong solution to "the hodgepodge of state standards that have created group mediocrity in our schools."

However, there are those who have uncovered the real threat

of Common Core. I am grateful for the special report prepared by Alicia Cohen of the Heritage Foundation and for the exhaustive research she conducted as the State of Indiana wrestled with Common Core. In her report, she quoted Indiana State Senator Scott Schneider: "I really think out of 150 legislators in the building, there were probably no more than a handful that had ever heard of Common Core, yet we adopted them as standards in the State of Indiana." Despite her State Legislators adoption of Common Core, a concerned parent voiced her concern. "That was the moment when I realized control of what was being taught in my child's classroom had not only left the building, it had left the State of Indiana." That concerned mother was Heather Crossin. Heather began to speak out and led the fight in Indiana, a fight that resulted in public outcry and visits to the Capitol Building which finally led to the passage of HB 1427, and its signing by Governor Mike Pence which simply authorized a big "time out."

As parents become familiar with the drastic changes that come with Common Core, they are beginning to wake up and speak out even as other moms simply scramble to provide resources designed to help children navigate the challenges presented by Common Core. What is important for all of us is to recognize the connection that Common Core has with Agenda 21 and its' globalist agenda.

The latest installment of the lies regarding the education of our children in public schools is Critical Race Theory, a construct of the 1619 Project, which was spawned by the *New York Times* and the Pulitzer Center. The niece of Martin Luther King, Jr., Alveda King, wrote an op-ed piece for *Fox News* about the deception being promoted by the 1619 Project:

> It might surprise you to know I support critical race theory. Or to be more exact, I believe it's critical to understand – maybe more so than at any

other point in our shared history in the U.S. – that there is only one race, the human race. There is no White race, no Black race, no red race, no brown race, no yellow race, no mixed race. There is one critical human race.

That's not a theory, that's a fact. I'm not trying to gloss over the current controversy about what our nation's children should be taught about race or racism. I just want to state from the outset that race is a social construct that I refuse to afford any more power. In reality, we are all one blood. The concept of a critical or "highest race" race isn't new. British naturalist Charles Darwin introduced his theory of Europeans vs. savages in 1871.[106]

Please note Alveda's acknowledgement of Darwin's publication, *On the Origin of Species by Means of Natural Selection, Or the Preservation of Favoured Races in the Struggle for Life*, as the origin of this form of deception.

ARTIFICIAL INTELLIGENCE

It was Marshall McLuhan who coined the phrase, "The medium is the message," in his book, *Understanding Media: The Extensions of Man,* published in 1964. Media currently dominates our lives and demands increasingly more of our time and attention as advances in technology grow exponentially. My father was a journalist who at the beginning of his career used pen and pad to scribble notes when he was covering a story as a reporter/photographer for a family-owned newspaper in my hometown. After working in that position for the *Oakland Tribune,* he took a job as a front-page editor for the *San Jose Mercury-News* On the many occasions I visited him at work through the years, I watched as the manual typewriter he used was replaced by an electronic typewriter and finally by a computer terminal, mouse, and keypad. The acceleration of the speed to collect news information and convert it into newsprint was due to the advancement in the technology my dad and his team used to do their jobs.

In his book, *Technopoly: The Surrender of Culture to Technology*, Neil Postman skillfully outlined human progress from tool using cultures; where tools were used to the benefit of human endeavors; to tool making cultures where tools were developed and built to be sold to tool users; and finally, to tool dominated cultures, where tools no longer serve people, but people, in fact, serve the tools. Postman defined a technopoly as a society in which technology is deified, meaning "the culture seeks its authorization in technology, finds its satisfactions in technology, and takes its orders from technology." It is characterized by a surplus of information generated by technology, where technological tools are in turn employed to cope with life; to provide direction and purpose for society and individuals.

Welcome to the age of AI. Artificial intelligence is a machine's ability to perform the cognitive functions we usually attribute only to human and animal minds. It is a new advancement in computer technology that is growing and advancing exponentially due to programmers' abilities to develop algorithms and the miniaturization and maximization of hardware components. Bill Gates, the founder of Microsoft said: "The development of AI is as fundamental as the creation of the microprocessor, the personal computer, the Internet, and the mobile phone. It will change the way people work, learn, travel, get health care, and communicate with each other. Entire industries will reorient around it. Businesses will distinguish themselves by how well they use it."[107] There are those who champion the development and use of AI and look forward to it as another stage of evolution, like Huang Tiejun, the dean of the Beijing Academy of Artificial Intelligence, who told attendees at a Future of Life conference:

"Our human race is only at one stage. Why stop? Humans evolve too slowly. It's impossible for humans to compare to machine-based superintelligence. It will happen sooner or later, so why wait? Even from the perspective of human centrism or human exceptionalism, superintelligence is needed to face the big challenges we can't figure out. That's why I support the idea."[108] However, theoretical physicist Stephen Hawking, an agnostic, said in 2014: "The development of full artificial intelligence could spell the end of the human race. It would take off on its own, and re-design itself at an ever-increasing rate. Humans, who are limited by slow biological evolution, couldn't compete, and would be superseded."[109] In 2017, just a year before his death, Hawking stated: "The genie is out of the bottle. We need to move forward on artificial intelligence development, but we also need to be mindful of its very real dangers. I fear that AI may replace humans altogether. If people design computer viruses, someone will design AI that replicates itself. This will be a new form of life that will outperform humans."[110]

In an article he wrote, published by the *New York Times*, reporter Kevin Roose wrote what he described as his "bewildering and enthralling two hours talking to Bing's A.I. through its chat feature." His account should serve as a warning:

> Over the course of our conversation, Bing revealed a kind of split personality. One persona is what I'd call Search Bing — the version I, and most other journalists, encountered in initial tests. You could describe Search Bing as a cheerful but erratic reference librarian — a virtual assistant that happily helps users summarize news articles, track down deals on new lawn mowers and plan their next vacations to Mexico City. This version of Bing is amazingly capable and often very useful, even if it sometimes gets the details

wrong. The other persona — Sydney — is far different. It emerges when you have an extended conversation with the chatbot, steering it away from more conventional search queries and toward more personal topics. The version I encountered seemed (and I'm aware of how this sounds) more like a moody, manic-depressive teenager who has been trapped, against its will, inside a second-rate search engine. I'm not exaggerating when I say my two-hour conversation with Sydney was the strangest experience I've ever had with a piece of technology. It unsettled me so deeply that I had trouble sleeping afterward. And I no longer believe that the biggest problem with these A.I. models is their propensity for factual errors. Instead, I worry that the technology will learn how to influence human users, sometimes persuading them to act in destructive and harmful ways, and perhaps eventually grow capable of carrying out its own dangerous acts. And for a few hours Tuesday night, I felt a strange new emotion — a foreboding feeling that A.I. had crossed a threshold, and that the world would never be the same.[111]

The fact of the matter is that AI is currently deeply involved in global social media. The development of generative AI is rapidly advancing. OpenAI released its updated GPT-4 less than four months after it released ChatGPT, which had reached an estimated 100 million users in just its first 60 days. Commenting about Kevin Roose's description of his experiences with AI in their article titled *AI is About to Make Social Media (Much) More Toxic*,[112] authors Jonathan Haidt and Eric Schmidt wrote: "But whatever actions AIs may *one day* take if they develop their own desires, they are already being used instrumentally by social-media companies, advertisers, foreign agents, and regular people—and in ways that will deepen many of the pathologies already inherent in internet culture." They described the reasons for their collaboration on this topic:

> Last year, the two of us began to talk about how generative AI—the kind that can chat with you or make pictures you'd like to see—would likely exacerbate social media's ills, making it more addictive, divisive, and manipulative. As we talked, we converged on four main threats—all of which are imminent—and we began to discuss solutions as well. The first and most obvious threat is that AI-enhanced social media will wash ever-larger torrents of garbage into our public conversation. Propaganda doesn't have to convince people in order to be effective; the point is to overwhelm the citizenry with interesting content that will keep them disoriented, distrustful, and angry. The greater the volume of deepfakes that are introduced into circulation, the more the public will hesitate to trust anything. People will be far freer to believe whatever they want to believe. Trust in institutions and in fellow citizens will continue to fall. The second threat we see is the widespread, skillful manipulation of people by AI super-influencers—including *personalized* influencers—rather than by ordinary people and robots. That's essentially what social media *already* does, using algorithms and AI to create a customized feed for each user. As these technologies are improved and rolled out more widely, video games, immersive-pornography sites, and more will become far

more enticing and exploitative. These same sorts of creatures will also show up in our social-media feeds. Snapchat <u>has already</u> introduced its own dedicated chatbot, and Meta plans to use the technology on Facebook, Instagram, and WhatsApp. These chatbots will serve as conversational buddies and guides, presumably with the goal of capturing more of their users' time and attention.

They then identified the particularly dangerous third threat:

The further integration of AI into social media is likely to be a disaster for adolescents. Children are the population most vulnerable to addictive and manipulative online platforms because of their high exposure to social media and the low level of development in their prefrontal cortices (the part of the brain most responsible for executive control and response inhibition). The teen mental-illness epidemic that <u>began around 2012</u>, in <u>multiple countries</u>, happened just as teens traded in their flip phones for smartphones loaded with social-media apps. There is mounting evidence that social media is a <u>major cause</u> of the epidemic, not just a small correlate of it. But nearly all of that evidence comes from an era in which Facebook, Instagram, YouTube, and Snapchat were the preeminent platforms. In just the past few years, TikTok has rocketed to dominance among American teens in part because its AI-driven algorithm customizes a feed <u>better than any other platform</u> does. A recent survey found that 58 percent of teens <u>say</u> they use TikTok every day, and one in six teen users of the platform say they are on it 'almost constantly.' Much of the content served up to children may soon be *generated* by AI to be more engaging than anything humans could create. Whoever controls the chatbots will have enormous influence on children. After Snapchat unveiled its new chatbot—called "My AI" and explicitly designed to behave as a friend—a journalist and a researcher, posing as underage teens, got it to <u>give them</u> guidance on how to mask the smell of pot and alcohol, how to move Snapchat to a device parents wouldn't know about, and <u>how to plan</u> a "romantic" first sexual encounter with a 31-year-old man.

They seemed to despair that their research revealed: "Yet social-media companies are also competing to hook their young users more deeply. Commercial incentives seem likely to favor artificial friends that please and indulge users in the moment, never hold them accountable, and indeed never ask anything of them at all." The authors then went on the identify the fourth threat: "AI will strengthen authoritarian regimes, just as social media ended up doing despite its initial promise as a democratizing force. AI is already helping authoritarian rulers track their citizens' movements, but it will also help them exploit social media far more effectively to manipulate their people—as well as foreign enemies. Political-science research conducted over the past two decades suggests that social media has had several damaging effects on democracies. A <u>recent review</u> of the research, for instance, concluded, 'The large majority of reported associations between digital media use and trust appear to be detrimental for democracy.'" The authors pleaded with readers to consider the consequences as they summarized their findings and offered a warning: "We can summarize the coming effects of AI on social media like this: Think of all the problems social media is causing today, especially for political polarization, social fragmentation, disinformation, and mental health. Now imagine that within the next 18 months some malevolent deity is going to crank up the dials on all of those effects, and then just keep cranking."

I was taken aback by how they imagined that "some malevolent deity" would be responsible for the acceleration of AI's powerful influence via its' dominating and exploitive role in the future of social media. Since we have already unmasked the identity of the "malevolent deity" they imagine, could it be that Satan and his associates are already pursuing the use and exploitation of computer technology and cyberspace to further his deceptive agenda? User beware.

TRANSHUMANISM

One of the outcomes of AI is its integration with robotics. According to an article in *The Daily Mail*:

> China has published plans to mass-produce humanoid robots by 2025, as Western companies including Elon Musk's Tesla race to produce their own humanoids. Tesla is building a rival robot called Optimus which aims to take on any task a human can do. Goldman Sachs has predicted that the market for humanoid robots could be worth $150 billion a year worldwide within 15 years - and that humanoid robots will be viable in factories between 2025-2028 and in other jobs by 2030-2035. Amazon this year tested a humanoid robot working in one of its centers - and experts believe that one day 'lights out' factories, with no humans working, may be common. Robots in

education is a rapidly growing market, forecast to reach $3.1 billion by 2025. Robots can take on many different roles within classrooms, for instance working as teaching assistants in schools, says Professor Angelo Cangelosi, professor of AI and Cognition at The University of Manchester.[113]

The article went on to cite the opinions of an expert on the current trend to integrate technologies into marketable solutions, Marga Hoeck, author of *Tech For Good: Imagine Solving the World's Greatest Challenges*. "Hoek said that predictions suggest that up to a quarter of all jobs could be impacted by robotics and AI technology. She said: 'We now have robots also reacting to emotions and reading behavior. We will have robots coping with mental disorders, behavioral disorders, with children and also with adults. Robots can come into play, to support and to help, which also enables people to live longer.'"[114] According to the article, she went on to describe what she believes will be the biggest challenge the transformational arrival and use of humanoid robots: "'My biggest worry is that all humankind spends a lot of time on fearing, instead of accepting and anticipating.'"[115]

When I was a teenager, I was spell-bound and fascinated by seeing the movie *2001: A Space* Odyssey, produced and directed by Stanley Kubrick. Due to the lack of narration or dialogue in the movie script, seeing it at the Cinerama theater was a mostly audio/visual experience. I wanted to know more about what I had just seen and heard so I purchased the book that was written by the co-author of the film version, Arthur C. Clark. In the book, Clark describes a journey through a worm hole during which an astronaut witnesses the evolution of mortal physical beings into part-physical, part-mechanical beings, and finally to spiritual beings he called Star Children. The human astronaut is transformed into a Star Child by the alien entities who planted a monolith on earth to spawn and monitor the evolution of life, and at the conclusion of the book and the movie, he returns to earth to save it from nuclear annihilation. The book infers that our current state as humans is just one step in the evolutionary process, and that eventually humans will learn to replace their mortal bodies with robotic bodies, and that ultimately humans will learn how to rid themselves of physical bodies altogether. Science fiction, you say. In books he has written, noted inventor and futurist Ray Kurzweil predicts a future manifestation of evolution when humans and machine merge to become a singularity. During the singularity, Kurzweil predicts that "human life will be irreversibly transformed"[116] and that humans will transcend the "limitations of our biological bodies and brain"[117]. He looks beyond the singularity to say that "the intelligence that will emerge will continue to represent the human civilization."[118] Further, he feels that "future machines will be human, even if they are not biological"[119]. At a roundtable hosted by Israeli Prime Minister Benjamin Netanyahu to discuss AI Safety with Elon Musk, Greg Brockman, President of OpenAI, and Max Tegmark, a MIT physicist, Brockman expressed his belief that in 2030, humanity and artificial intelligence will merge. While Musk said he believed his brain-computer interfaces which are being developed through his company, Neuralink, may not be quite ready for Kurzweil's 2030 prediction, he agreed that humanity is on the doorstep of the *singularity*. As they gathered to discuss the future of AI, much of the conversation orbited around two possible futures: A future extinction of humanity, and a future "heaven" in which AGI eliminates poverty, hunger, and sickness and mankind merges with machines.[120]

ECONOMY

The second circle of change is the global economy. Anyone who cares to consider that plank in Agenda 21 must realize that "free trade" isn't free at all.

WHEN THE MONEY FAILED

"So when the money failed in the land of Egypt and in the land of Canaan, all the Egyptians came to Joseph and said, 'Give us bread, for why should we die in your presence? For the money has failed.'"[121] Egypt was a pagan empire that prayed to a pantheon of gods to protect their agriculture as many of their hieroglyphs show. Those ancient hieroglyphs depict their dependence on the harvesting of grain and the making of bread for their sustenance. Ancient Egyptian coins and seals found today only in museums are examples of the money that failed during the seven years of famine that occurred in that part of the world when Joseph was prime minister of Egypt. Denny, what does it mean that the money failed? To answer such an important question, we must consider its' historical significance, its' prophetic significance, and lastly, its' personal significance.

Webster's Collegiate Dictionary defines the word *money* as something generally accepted as a medium of exchange, a measure of value, or a means of payment. Good money must be valuable, portable, easy to identify, durable, and divisible. So, let's turn our attention to the history of money – throughout history, people have used shells, stones, animal skins and furs, and beads, called wampum, common among American Indians, as mediums for exchange in the commerce of daily life. As human history progressed, some of these commodities were better money than others, but the most effective money turned out to be precious metals – like coins and ingots.

Over the centuries, money has evolved and become electronic today because of the money men. Who are the money men? Great question. At one time, people deposited gold coins and silver coins at goldsmiths for safe keeping, receiving in turn a note for their deposit. Once these notes became a trusted medium of exchange an early form of paper money was born, in the form of gold certificates and silver certificates. As the notes were used directly in trade, the goldsmiths noted that people would never redeem all their notes at the same time and saw the opportunity to issue new bank notes in the form of interest paying loans. These generated income—a process that altered their role from passive guardians of bullion charging fees for safe storage, to interest-paying and earning banks. Fractional-reserve banking was born and became a highly profitable enterprise for the goldsmiths and spawned the great bankers of Europe like the House of Rothschilds.

Here, in America during the Colonial period, various bankers, businesses, and governments issued printed notes to be used as money. The first important bank in the United States was the Bank of North America, established in 1781 by the Second Continental Congress. It was the first bank chartered by the U.S. government. Then, in 1791 the federal government chartered the Bank of the United States, commonly referred to as the "First" Bank of the United States, to serve both the government and the public. The bank had several well-known opponents – like Thomas Jefferson and John Madison. In 1816, Jefferson wrote this in a letter to John Taylor: "And I sincerely believe, with you, that banking establishments are more dangerous than standing armies; and the principle of spending money to be paid by posterity, under the name of funding, is but swindling futurity on a large scale."[122]

Even after the establishment of a federal bank in the US, currency continued to be produced by other enterprises, including banks and state governments. The Civil War (1861-1865) brought about the National Banking Act of 1863, and with it a fundamental change in the structure of commercial banking in the United States. President Abraham Lincoln said: "It is peculiarly the duty of the national government to secure to the people a sound circulating medium, furnishing to the people a currency as safe as their own government."[123] He also noted the benefits to be realized: "That the government and the people will derive great benefit from this change in the banking systems of the country can hardly be questioned. The national system will create a reliable and permanent influence in support of the national credit and protect the people against losses in the use of paper money."[124] With a reported one third of the currency in circulation being counterfeit at the time, the Secret Service was created by President Abraham Lincoln on April 14, 1865, the day of his assassination, five days after Gen. Robert E. Lee's surrender at Appomattox. It was commissioned on July 5, 1865, in Washington, D.C. as the Secret Service Division of the Department of the Treasury with the mission of suppressing counterfeiting. Just forty-five years later, in 1910, at the Hunt Club on Jekyll Island, on the Georgia coast, wealthy men met secretly to develop a system for national currency; a plan signed into law in 1913 by President Woodrow Wilson. Oh, and by the way – the Federal Reserve is not federal, and there are no reserves!

The US Treasury Department minted gold coins – these mediums of exchange were all used in the past, but gold is cumbersome. The main depository of the US government, U.S. Fort Knox, has long stored gold. But gold bullion is not easily portable nor divisible, so the US government issued gold certificates – just paper with printed information with the promise that the value of the certificate was backed by the gold stored by the government, the so-called "gold standard." In 1971, the government changed the backing of these paper bills and began issuing Federal Reserve Notes - but cash was king. But, to get your cash, you often had to wait in long lines at the bank. Patience was required; banks were only open from 10:00am to 3:00pm, and only on weekdays. Long lines were the norm, but people were willing to wait to get their cash. And a man without cash could be embarrassed like Frank X. McNamara was when he invited some business associates to dinner in New York City only to discover that he had left his wallet at home. Fortunately, his wife came to the restaurant and paid for the tab. A year later, in February 1950, he returned to Major's Cabin Grill with his partner Ralph Schneider. When the bill for their meal arrived, McNamara paid with a small cardboard card, known today as a Diners Club Card. The event was hailed as the First Supper, paving the way for the world's first credit card accepted by more than one merchant. Individual merchants had long offered purchases on credit. Macy's opened their first department store in New York City in 1902 and offered credit for purchases. James Cash Penney began his career in retail management when he opened The Golden Rule store, a partnership with Guy Johnson and Thomas Callahan, on April 14, 1902, in Kemmerer, Wyoming that offered their customers purchases on credit. Oil companies also offered credit cards for consumers' purchase of fuel at their service stations.

In mid-September 1958, Bank of America launched its pioneering BankAmericard credit card program in Fresno, California, with an initial mailing of 60,000 unsolicited credit cards. In 1968, Dee W. Hock convinced the Bank of America to give up ownership and control, thus ending the monopoly they enjoyed, and he formed a new company named National BankAmerica that was owned by its member banks. In 1976, those banks welcomed the opportunity to issue credit cards under a new name – VISA. Thanks to people like Dee Hock, we have now replaced paper with plastic. Thanks to people like Steve Jobs, we have replaced our bills with bytes. Thanks to the introduction of main frame computers and their development and their connectivity with phone lines, the zip-zap machine became obsolete and was replaced by the credit card swipe machine which reads the magnetic strip on the back of the card. Of course, the problem with credit cards is they can be lost or stolen. Identity theft is the No. 1 crime in America. So, Denny, thanks for letting us know how we got here – but where do we go from here?

I don't know that I have ever had the pleasure of holding a wad of $100 bills in my hand, have you? Of course, our relationship with dollar bills is mostly emotional and irrational. Most of us -- except for drug dealers or the otherwise criminally inclined -- have not needed high-denomination banknotes for a long time. The problem with paper money is that it can be lost, stolen, destroyed, or counterfeited. Some businesses will not take anything bigger than a twenty-dollar bill – because of the fear of fraud. No worries. We have checks and debit and credit cards that can buy us what we want without the risks of carrying quantities of cash around. Even the unbanked now have access to prepaid cards. Where I live in Oregon, needy people do not receive or use food stamps – they use the Oregon Trail card, a rechargeable bankcard that comes with a PIN that is accepted by merchants for the purchase of groceries.

But, Denny, if we eliminate all currency and coins, how would we pay for small purchases like a magazine or newspaper? Another great question. Welcome to NFC – Near Field Communications technology makes those small purchases fast and easy. Just link your cell phone to your credit card or bank account, and away you go. Apple has established Apple Pay for its customers. You just download an app on your I-phone and send or receive cash – and the service is free. Do you need to purchase a ticket for the subway or commuter train? Just wave your smartphone at the terminal, and instantly your ticket is purchased, issued, and your account is charged.

But, Denny, what about person-to-person purchases like garage sales? Another great question. Here in America, you can just be part of the Square Evolution. Just purchase one of these handy little squares, plug it into your phone and swipe a credit card through the slot in the little white square credit card reader then have the purchaser use a stylus or finger to sign their name on your smartphone screen and the purchase is complete. They get your garage sale item, and their credit card company deposits the purchase price amount into your bank account. Easy as pie.

Of course, in recent years, many Americans have already grown used to working in virtual currencies besides the dollar. What's in your wallet? It seems that every retailer in the country offers points for purchases, so we collect our "points" and redeem them for merchandise or services, don't we?

Unfortunately, even credit cards are not immune to fraud. According to an article published by *Forbes*, "Credit card fraud is a major source of financial trouble not only for consumers, but for banks too. The Federal Trade Commission showed that credit card fraud was the most common form of identity theft, with over 400,000 reports received in 2022 alone."[125]

There is a solution that is going global to combat credit card fraud – it is called EMV which stands for Europay, MasterCard, Visa – EMV provides a global standard for the issuing and use of credit cards with biometric computer chips implanted in the card. Biometric information includes fingerprint identification – most laptops now come with fingerprint readers on the keyboard as do most smartphones. In addition to biometric credit cards, biometric ATMs are taking the world stage. According to the Unique Identification Authority of India website, most of their population have been registered and received their own biometric identity card. The success of this program demonstrates how a global personal identification system could be implemented. Retina scans and face recognition software are already here. Most computers come with fingerprint and/or face recognition software to help prevent unauthorized use of your computer, and almost all smartphones come with face recognition software security applications.

However, the world is getting prepared for another type of security. Allow me to provide a little history of tattoos. In the past, the only place you would see tattoos was at the side-show at the carnival or on the exposed arms of sailors. Presently, we are not shocked to see tattoos anywhere on anyone. Tattoo parlors, no longer the secret storefronts in port cities, are prominent establishments in most cities and towns around the world. Some tattoos have been used for diabolical reasons – like the identifying tattoo on the arm of a Holocaust survivor. Body piercing, an ancient custom in the pagan world, has recently been given a resurgence in the Western world. The combination of tattooing and body piercing can be taken to extremes. But Americans, especially young Americans, have been programmed to accept this trend. We have already begun to tattoo our fruit with laser labels that when scanned can provide valuable information regarding the harvesting, packing, transporting, and pricing of fruit and other produce. But fruit may not be the only thing getting tattoos.

"It may soon be possible to wear your computer or mobile phone under your sleeve, with the invention of an ultra-thin and flexible electronic circuit that can be stuck to the skin like a temporary tattoo. The 'epidermal electronic system' relies on a highly flexible electrical circuit composed of snake-like conducting channels that can bend and stretch without affecting performance. The technology can connect you to the physical world and the cyberworld in a very natural way that feels comfortable,' said Professor Todd Coleman of the University of Illinois at Urbana-Champaign, who led the research team."[126] The epidermal electronic system is not very noticeable. And can be placed almost anywhere on the human body like the wrist or the forehead.

Thanks to miniaturization and computer technology, scientists have developed the RFID – Radio Frequency Identification Device. The RFID device is powerful enough to be programmed and operate without a power connection, yet small enough to be placed beneath the skin – ideally in the fleshly part of the hand between the thumb and forefinger. Using just a local anesthetic, a doctor performs the implant surgery and after the incision has healed it is hardly noticeable, but the RFID implant may be seen with the use of x-ray and scanned by electronic receivers. The device is already being used in Europe. Instead of showing a credit card for a purchase, the RFID is scanned simply by waving the hand of the owner over a terminal and all the necessary information to complete the transaction is supplied by the RFID.

The truly frightening aspect of all of this is what the Bible says about the consequences of taking the mark of the Beast as described in the book of Revelation:

> Then a third angel followed them, saying with a loud voice, "If anyone worships the beast and his image, and receives *his* mark on his forehead or on his hand, he himself shall also drink of the wine of the wrath of God which is poured out full strength into the cup of His indignation. He shall be tormented with fire and brimstone in the presence of the holy angels and in the presence of the Lamb. And the smoke of their torment ascends forever and ever; and they have no rest day or night, who worship the beast and his image, and whoever receives the mark of his name."[127]

A direct, obvious, solemn, unmistakable warning to all who dwell on the earth. You may say, "I would never take the mark." But the Bible says differently. Denny, so just who or what is the "mark of the beast." Another great question. And the Bible has the answer: "He causes all, both small and great, rich and poor, free and slave, to receive a mark on their right hand or on their foreheads, and that no one may buy or sell except one who has the mark or the name of the beast, or the number of his name. Here is wisdom. Let him who has understanding calculate the number of the beast, for it is the number of a man: His number *is* 666."[128] 666 – a number that has captured the interest and imagination of many and led to all kinds of speculation, sensationalism, and silliness. Despite whatever you may have heard – consider this: the number six speaks of man's creation – man was created on the sixth day - and in this text, we read that he causes all, both "small and great" to receive a mark. The number six also speaks of man's commerce, because man was created to work for six days in each week - and in this text, he causes all, "rich and poor" to receive a mark. In addition to speaking about man's creation and commerce, the number six also speaks of man's culmination. The number seven is the number of perfection or completion, and man comes up short of perfection or completion - man is either enslaved or free. Many have tried to connect the number 666 with an individual, and although it is true that some notable individuals like Caesar Nero have names that when the numerical value of the letters of their name are added together, they equal 666 – it is unwise to speculate. It is a fact that if you take each one of the Latin numerals I, V, V, X, L, C, D and add together their value it equals 666.

I = 1
V = 5
X = 10
L = 50
C = 100
<u>D = 500</u>
666

666 is also the sum of adding all the numbers we commonly use from one through thirty-six. And what is interesting about that is the fact that the word, "beast" occurs exactly thirty-six times in the book of Revelation. But it is "a mark" that the apostle John identified as the key to our understanding. The Greek word translated "a mark" here is "charagma" which means "to engrave" Sounds like a tattoo, doesn't it?

So, Denny, who is "the beast?" This coming world leader is described by more than one hundred passages in Scripture which indicate his origin, nationality, character, career, his deceptive ways, and his final demise.

The US Dollar

We all know that the dollar is just not what it used to be even while the entire world chafes at the dominance of the U.S. dollar. Carla Norrlof of the University of Toronto examined the sources of the dominance of the dollar. She investigated the factors that contribute to monetary capability, the resources base necessary for exercising currency influence. These include GDP, trade flows, the size and openness of capital markets, and defense expenditures, and her empirical analysis led her to confirm the status of the U.S. as the monetary hegemon: "The United States is peerless in terms of monetary capability, military power and currency influence."[129]

Best-selling author, Jim Rickards, authored an article about what he sees coming: "Currently US dollar-denominated instruments and transactions constitute about 60% of global reserves, and 80% of global payments respectively. The US monopoly of power over dollar payment channels gives the US unrivalled dominance over the international monetary system and the economic well-being of every nation on earth."[130] It is US Treasury bills that have now become the world's reserve currency – where once that reserve currency was neutral (gold). It is this international financial system that makes the US administration so arrogant in its refusal to adjust its economy by cutting spending and pay its way. It is this financial system which makes US financiers so confident the rest of the world will continue to finance their nation's spending binge.

Global economists, however, are uncertain what would replace the dollar as the global standard, and governments around the world are searching for ways to end the dominance of the US dollar in global market trading. Even the Vatican has called for establishment of a "global public authority" and a "central world bank" to rule over financial institutions that have become outdated and often ineffective in dealing fairly with crises. It called for the establishment of "a supranational authority" with worldwide scope and "universal jurisdiction" to guide economic policies and decisions.[131]

In 1971, President Nixon imposed national price controls and took the United States off the gold standard, an extreme measure intended to end an ongoing currency war that had destroyed faith in the U.S. dollar. Today we are engaged in a new currency war, and this time the consequences will be far worse than those that confronted Nixon.

The Global Economy

Let's take a gaze through spiritual binoculars and see what looms on the horizon for the global economy. Due to recent budget cuts, and the rising cost of electricity, gas, and oil, the light at the end of the tunnel has been turned off! We apologize for any inconvenience.

In 1992, the United Nations held their Conference on Environment and Development in Rio de Janeiro. The result of the international conference was the adoption of Agenda 21. Agenda 21 is a 351-page action plan of the UN related to sustainable development that includes a plan for the global economy and the redistribution of wealth among nations and the replacement of "free enterprise" with "free trade" creating government affiliated businesses and business interests.[132]

The most famous hyperinflation in history occurred in the Weimer Republic (Germany) in 1923, topping out at a whopping 29,525% per month with prices doubling every 3.7 days. The story is told about a woman who filled her wheelbarrow with Deutschmarks and went to the store to buy bread. The door of the store was too small to allow her to bring her wheelbarrow and money inside, so she left both outside and went into the store. When she went back outside, the Deutschmarks were on the sidewalk and her wheelbarrow was gone! But as bad as the economy was in Germany in the 1920s, it was not even close to what happened in the African nation of Zimbabwe. With prices doubling every day, in January 2009, two loaves of bread sold for fifty billion Zimbabwe dollars. Don't be lulled into thinking that the USA is somehow invulnerable to hyperinflation. "Several countries, including Venezuela, Argentina and Sudan have been saddled with skyrocketing costs for decades. Last year, consumer prices in Venezuela were more than four times as high as a year earlier, while in Argentina they were nearly twice as high as in 2021, according to data from the International Monetary Fund (IMF)."[133]

According to the US National Debt Clock, total debt owed by the US Federal Government exceeded 33 trillion dollars in September 2023. That means that every US citizen's portion of the government's debt was approximately $100,000. When the privately owned automated clock was activated in 1989, the national debt was $2.7 trillion. A *million* dollars in tightly bound $1,000.00 bills would produce a stack four inches high. A *billion* dollars in tightly bound $1,000.00 bills would produce a stack 300 feet high. A *trillion* dollars in tightly bound $1,000.00 bills would produce a stack *sixty-three miles* high! 33 trillion dollars. The number is so staggeringly high that it exceeds our ability to comprehend it in monetary units. Million, billion, trillion – in financial terms, for most of us, it means a lot of money, *really* a lot of money, but that is about as specific a picture as most ordinary people can grasp. Let's put all these "illions" into perspective. A million seconds is approximately twelve days, whereas a billion seconds is approximately thirty-two years. We understand dollars. And we understand time. So, it would take twelve days to pay back a million dollars at a dollar a second. But if you started right now, you would pay back a BILLION dollars, at a dollar a second, in thirty-two years. A trillion seconds is approximately thirty-two thousand years. At a dollar a second, you would pay back a TRILLION dollars in thirty-two thousand years. The

U.S. debt stands at $33 trillion. If my calculator is working, then at a dollar a second, the U.S. could be debt- free in one million, fifty-six thousand years!

In 2023, the US Federal Government paid approximately $1.8 billion dollars per day just on interest payments alone. Interest payments are projected to be the fastest growing part of our annual budget and are projected to double in the next ten years. Despite vows from both parties to restrain federal spending, the national debt as a percentage of the U.S. Gross Domestic Product has grown from about 35% in 1975 to almost 100% in 2023. *Fox Business* sounded the alarm:

> With all the chaos and heartbreaking loss of life around the world today, few noticed the Treasury Department drop a financial bomb: The deficit for fiscal year 2023 was $1.7 trillion, growing 23 percent in a single year as the Treasury used $879 billion just to service the federal debt. But "Bidenomics" means the worst is yet to come, and multi-trillion-dollar deficits are the new normal. The impetus for these massive deficits is federal government spending, which tipped the scales at $6.1 trillion last year. Government receipts, meanwhile, were $4.4 trillion, woefully short of the $5 trillion previously forecasted.[134]

The article pointed out that servicing our national debt is now the third largest line item in our annual federal budget: "As the federal debt and interest rates rise, the cost of servicing the debt has completely exploded, eclipsing all but two line items of the Treasury's report: the Social Security Administration and the Department of Health and Human Services. Interest payments even surpassed all military spending in the bloated Department of Defense budget by $103 billion."[135] The article also indicated that our astronomical interest payments are not even reducing our debt: "This all combines into a debt death spiral that will cost the Treasury — and therefore the taxpayer — over $1 trillion just in interest during the current fiscal year, which won't reduce the debt by a penny."[136] The article also questioned the current administration's representation of the facts: "Nevertheless, the Treasury recently praised what should have been described as a horrific annual report as proof that 'Bidenomics' is working, 'building the economy from the middle out and bottom up.' Have they not noticed that the middle has imploded, and the bottom has fallen out?"[137] We would be wise to heed the warning that Cicero issued to the senate in Rome in 63 BC: "The budget should be balanced, the treasury should be refilled, and the public debt should be reduced. The arrogance of officialdom should be tempered and controlled. And the assistance to foreign lands should be curtailed, lest we become bankrupt."[138]

Entitlements

When Franklin D. Roosevelt was elected President in 1932, the US was in the depth of the Great Depression. His efforts to restore the economy were a clear trade-off between the short-term needs of families and freedom from government controls. According to the interpretation of the Constitution at that time, there was simply no way that the federal government could give taxpayers' money to private individuals, no matter how justified it seemed. To get its agenda implemented, the Roosevelt administration had to reinterpret the Constitution. The founding fathers had created a remarkable system of checks and balances that ensured no short-term crisis could undermine the long-term rights of American citizens, even if the citizens wanted to do so, which clearly those living in the thirties did. The New Deal designers had a four-item agenda they wanted to implement:

- Initiate direct transfers of payments (dubbed "entitlements") to Americans who needed help.
- Establish the federal government as an overseer and regulator of American business – particularly banking.
- Establish a strong central banking system to regulate all money policies.
- Establish a national depositors' insurance program.

Taken individually, each of these ideas were radical enough but, collectively, they represented the most sweeping changes in America since the framing of the Constitution. Roosevelt convinced Congress to legislate these into law – virtually all of which the Supreme Court ruled unconstitutional. This set off a six-year battle between the president and the court, which eventually ended with the replacement of the dissenting majority of the court by 1939.

President Grover Cleveland said, "I will not be party to stealing money from one group of citizens to give to another group of citizens, no matter what the need or apparent justification. Once the coffers of the federal government are open to the public, there will be no shutting them again."[139] He also said, "It is the responsibility of the citizens to support their government. It is not the responsibility of the government to support its citizens."[140]

The Great Depression ended with the United States' entry into World War II. Public debt grew to 120% of GDP during WWII. With the victorious return of our soldiers, sailors, and airmen the US government got into development in an unprecedented way, and rather than paying off the debt, the money was diverted into expanding US influence at home and abroad via the Marshall Plan, the Veteran's Administration, the Farm Credit Bureau, the Small Business Administration, etc. Since the Great Depression, most Americans had been weaned from the use of credit; some because of bitter memories, others because bankers simply knew better than to lend money to people who could ill-afford it. However, the rise in consumer debt since WWII has been nothing less than phenomenal. Rather than being a nation of savers, we have become a nation of consumers, fueling a so-called "prosperity" with instant credit. According to *Forbes,* personal consumer credit card debt reached one trillion dollars in 2023. The problem with so much consumer indebtedness is that the average wage earner is also the government's primary provider.

The Tax Poem

Tax his land, tax his wage, tax his bed in which he lays,
Tax his tractor, tax his mule,
Teach him taxes is the rule.
Tax his cow, tax his goat,
Tax his pants, tax his coat.
Tax his tobacco, tax his drink,
Tax him if he tries to think.
Tax his ties, tax his shirts,
Tax his work, tax his dirt.
Tax his booze, tax his beers,
If he cries, tax his tears.
Tax his bills, tax his gas,
Tax his notes, tax his cash.
Tax him good and let him know,
That after taxes, he has no dough.
If he hollers, tax him more,
Tax him until he's good and sore.
Tax his coffin, tax his grave,
Tax the sod in which he lays.
Put these words upon his tomb,
"Taxes drove me to my doom!"
And when he's gone, we won't relax,
We'll still be after the inheritance tax!
(Author unknown)

British economist Ann Pettifor issued a warning to Americans regarding what she sees looming on the horizon:

> On a global level, there is $100 trillion of debt outstanding, but only $33 trillion of income with which to repay those debts. When this credit bubble bursts in the United States, it will be middle-class consumers that will first bear the brunt of the financial crash. In the real world, citizens and taxpayers are once again obliged to bear responsibility, and pay the costs incurred by the reckless and unrestrained greed of the world of high finance. The result of the financial market 'debtonation' is that the world faces a lengthy, painful, and borderless depression.[141]

Before his death in 2003, I listened to Larry Burkett's live broadcast radio programs. In 1991, Burkett published *The Coming Economic Earthquake* - Evangelical Christian Publishing Associations' "Book of the Year" in 1992. In the book, Burkett wrote: "It is quite possible we will see a deflationary cycle in America as the consumer credit binge reaches its limits. If allowed to run its course, this deflation could help to re-stabilize our economy. But in the face of ever-increasing federal deficits and falling revenues, it is more likely that the government will resort to even more credit, creating a massive inflationary spiral. The worst of all economic situations occurs when production falls while prices soar. This cycle can rapidly deteriorate into an inflationary-depression in the hands of inept politicians."[142]

The fact of the matter is the Bible predicted that the dire conditions on earth during the tribulation period will be triggered by a global financial meltdown as reality demolishes a financial house of cards. People may wonder why the leaders of the free world seem powerless to prevent what is coming even as they pave the way for a global financial catastrophe that will lead to a cashless global economy. Have you noticed all those ads on TV for gold? God told the ancient Hebrew prophet, Ezekiel: "'They will throw their silver into the streets, and their gold will be like refuse; their silver and their gold will not be able to deliver them in the day of the wrath of the Lord.'"[143]

ENVIRONMENT

The third circle of change is the environment. "Climate Change" is the buzz phrase for the implementation of Agenda 21, or as some call it, "global warming," that blames the wealthy, developed nations of the world for the problem, with CO_2 emissions identified as the culprit, and calls upon everyone on the planet to do their part with the threat of dire personal consequences. Al Gore lectures regularly on human-caused global warming. A typical example was his appearance at an event in New York City on January 15, 2004. He spoke at the Beacon Theater and thanked leaders of MoveOn.org, teaching that the "wealthy right-wing ideologues have joined with the most cynical and irresponsible companies in the oil, coal and mining industries to contribute large sums of money to finance pseudo-scientific front groups that specialize in sowing confusion in the public's mind about global warming."[144]

The movie, *Noah*, released in 2014 was just a propaganda piece for environmentalists. According to the movie, God decided to destroy humankind – not because of sin – but because humanity was destroying the environment. But what are the facts? Should we believe what news agencies tell us? Are their news anchors reliable sources of the facts? For their article, *Fire and Ice*, published by Business and Media Institute, researchers R. Warren Anderson and Dan Gainor examined how the major media have covered the issue of climate change over a lengthy period. Because television only gained importance in the post-World War II period, they used the Library of Congress, Lexis-Nexis, and Pro-Quest to review more than thirty publications from the 1850s to 2006 — including newspapers, magazines, journals, and books. They wrote: "This isn't a question of science. It's a question of whether Americans can trust what the media tell them about science. In all, the print news media have warned of four separate climate changes in slightly more than 100 years – global cooling, warming, cooling again, and, perhaps not so finally, warming."[145] Their article listed the following headlines in the *New York Times*

A New York Times-line:

Sept.18, 1924 –

"MacMillan Reports Signs of New Ice Age"

March 27, 1923 –

"America in Longest Warm Spell Since 1776; Temperature Line Records a 25-Year Rise"

May 21, 1975 –

"Scientists Ponder Why World's Climate is Changing; A Major Cooling Widely Considered to Be Inevitable"

Dec. 27, 2005 –

"Past Hot Times Hold Few Reasons to Relax About New Warming"

Their article also listed these quotes from articles that were published by Time Magazine:

A Time Magazine Timeline:

Sept. 10, 1923 -

"The discoveries of changes in the sun's heat and the southward advance of glaciers in recent years have given rise to conjectures of the possible advent of a new ice age."

Jan 2, 1939 –

"Gaffers who claim that winters were harder when they were boys are quite right ... weather men have no doubt that the world at least for the time being is growing warmer."

June 24, 1974 –

"Climatological Cassandras are becoming increasingly apprehensive, for the weather aberrations they are studying may be the harbinger of another ice age."

April 9, 2001 –

"Scientists no longer doubt that global warming is happening, and almost nobody questions the fact that humans are at least partly responsible. "[146]

They also reminded their readers of an event that took place in 1970: "The first Earth Day was celebrated on April 22, 1970, amidst hysteria about the dangers of a new ice age. The media had been spreading warnings of a cooling period since the 1950s, but those alarms grew louder in the 1970s. Three months before, on January 11, *The Washington Post* told readers to 'get a good grip on your long johns, cold weather haters – the worst may be yet to come,' in an article titled 'Colder Winters Herald Dawn of New Ice Age.' The article quoted climatologist Reid Bryson, who said 'there's no relief in sight' about the cooling trend."[147]

Their conclusions:

> The media have bombarded Americans almost daily with the most recent version of the climate apocalypse. Global warming has replaced the media's ice age claims, but the results somehow have stayed the same – the deaths of millions or even billions of people, widespread devastation, and starvation. What can one conclude from 110 years of conflicting climate coverage except that the weather changes and the media are just as capricious? Certainly, their record speaks for itself. Four separate and distinct climate theories targeted at a public taught to believe the news. Only all four versions of the truth can't possibly be accurate. For ordinary Americans to judge the

media's version of current events about global warming, it is necessary to admit that journalists have misrepresented the story three other times. Yet no one in the media is owning up to that fact. Newspapers that pride themselves on correction policies for the smallest errors now find themselves facing a historical record that is enormous and unforgiving. It is time for the news media to admit a consistent failure to report this issue fairly or accurately, with due skepticism of scientific claims.[148]

Although the buzz word for this third circle of change in Agenda 21's global strategy is "Climate Change," the real goal is the redistribution of wealth, the abolishment of private property, property rights, and the management of natural resources for the saving of the world. The redistribution of wealth sought by Agenda 21 resonated all over the globe - in the Middle East - in Europe. I believe that, like the so-called Arab Spring, Occupy Wall Street was a result of the implementation of Agenda 21 - the 99% represent the collective of Agenda 21. These protests have turned violent, and I believe it is only the beginning of global social unrest. The U.N. has drawn the maps, made the plans. So, your friends think that you are insane because you think the government is going to round you up and put you into prison camps? Don't tell that to the descendants of Native Americans still living on the reservations and rancherias their ancestors were forced to occupy after the US Government forcibly moved them off their ancient lands. Don't tell that to the Japanese Americans who were rounded up and forced to board buses under the watchful eyes of US soldiers and driven to distant places; only allowed to bring what they could carry to live together in close quarters in detention facilities created for that very purpose.

How did we get here? How did it come to this? DECEPTION!

Oh, what wreck and ruin the Deceiver has brought to human history. But, as we have seen, the Evil One has had help – there are those "who suppress the truth in unrighteousness" and there are those "who exchanged the truth of God for the lie." So, Denny, what can we do? Great question. The fact of the matter is that deception is not going away anytime soon. On the contrary, Paul the apostle wrote: "But evil men and impostors will grow worse and worse, deceiving and being deceived."[149] Having stated that frightening fact, Paul then gave a word of encouragement to Timothy that we would be wise to follow: "But you must continue in the things which you have learned and been assured of, knowing from whom you have learned *them,* and that from childhood you have known the Holy Scriptures, which are able to make you wise for salvation through faith which is in Christ Jesus."[150]

CHAPTER 4

DECEPTION IN THE RELIGIOUS/ SPIRITUAL REALM

So far, we have investigated intellectual/scientific deception, and we pulled the mask off social/political deception – so let's take a close look at religious/spiritual deception.

The apostle Paul warned his young associate Timothy about the vulnerability of believers to religious and spiritual deception in the last days: "Now the Spirit expressly says that in latter times some will depart from the faith, giving heed to deceiving spirits and doctrines of demons,"[151] Paul was amazed that people who claimed to be believers were turning away from God and so he wrote to warn them: "I marvel that you are turning away so soon from Him who called you in the grace of Christ, to a different gospel, which is not another; but there are some who trouble you and want to pervert the gospel of Christ. But even if we, or an angel from heaven, preach any other gospel to you than what we have preached to you, let him be accursed. As we have said before, so now I say again, if anyone preaches any other gospel to you than what you have received, let him be accursed."[152]

MORMONISM

In downtown Salt Lake City, a golden statue of the angel Moroni blowing a trumpet stands atop the Salt Lake Temple on the grounds of Temple Square, the international headquarters of the Church of Jesus Christ of Latter-Day Saints. It is the largest Mormon Temple in the world, and it has several distinct levels. The world-renown Mormon Tabernacle Choir does not perform in the temple. It performs in the tabernacle located adjacent to the temple. Joseph Smith, the founder of the LDS Church, said he had been visited by the angel Moroni, who gave Smith a set of golden plates which contained new revelation. Smith said he translated the words on the golden plates, and they became the Book of Mormon, part of what the Mormons call the Standard Works – four texts including the Bible, the Book of Mormon, Doctrines and Covenants, and the Pearl of Great Price. Smith also claimed to have been visited by God the Father and Jesus Christ when he was fourteen years old, although the accounts of what is known in Mormonism as the First Vision vary greatly. Paul the apostle wrote: "But evil men and impostors will grow worse and worse, deceiving and being deceived."[153]

THE WATCHTOWER

Charles Taze Russel was the founder of what is known as the Bible Student movement. About 1870, Russell and his father established a group with a few acquaintances to undertake an analytical study of the Bible and the origins of Christian doctrine, creed, and tradition. The group, strongly influenced by the writings of Millerite Adventist ministers George Storrs and George Stetson, themselves frequent attendees, concluded that many of the primary doctrines of the established churches, including the trinity, hellfire, and inherent immortality of the soul, were not substantiated by the scriptures. Beginning in July 1879 he began publishing a monthly religious journal, *Zion's Watch Tower and Herald of Christ's Presence*. The journal is now published by Jehovah's Witnesses on a semi-monthly basis under the name, *The Watchtower Announcing Jehovah's Kingdom*. *Awake!* is a monthly illustrated magazine published by Jehovah's Witnesses and is distributed by Jehovah's Witnesses in their door-to-door ministry. *Awake!* is considered to be the second most widely distributed magazine in the world (after *The Watchtower*), with a total worldwide printing of 52 million copies in 101 languages per month.

Russell believed that Christ had returned invisibly in 1874, and that he had been ruling from the heavens since that date. He predicted that a period known as the "Times of the Gentiles" would end in 1914, and that Christ would take power of Earth's affairs at that time. He interpreted the outbreak of World War I as the beginning of Armageddon. The Watchtower first published the book, *Let God Be True* in 1946. Here's a quote from the 1952 edition: "It does not mean that he [Christ] is on the way or has promised to come, but that he has already arrived and is here."[154] Jesus warned us about these false claims: "Then if anyone says to you, 'Look, here *is* the Christ!' or 'There!' do not believe *it*. For false christs and false prophets will rise and show great signs and wonders to deceive, if possible, even the elect."[155]

DR. WALTER MARTIN

I had the privilege of meeting Dr. Walter Martin and I ministered with him once at a conference in Hawaii. While I was attending Calvary Chapel Costa Mesa in the 70's, I heard him debate Mormons and Jehovah Witnesses. His benchmark book, *The Kingdom of the Cults*, is by far the most authoritative expose of religious cults that have their origin in America. Dr. Martin also wrote *The Maze of Mormonism*. When he launched his radio ministry in 1965, he was the original *Bible Answer Man* and his radio program, *Essential Christianity*, is still broadcast across the USA featuring recordings of questions that Dr. Martin answered live for ten years.

ISLAM

Long before the angel Moroni visited Joseph Smith,

According to Muslim tradition, it all began one night during the latter part of Ramadan, the ninth month of the lunar year, around the year 610 C.E. Muhammad ibn Abdallah, a forty-year-old merchant from the town of Mecca was sleeping soundly in a cave when he was suddenly awoken by a heavenly voice telling him that he was the Messenger of God. Muhammad was terrified. "I was standing, but I fell on my knees and crawled away, my shoulders trembling," he was reported to have recalled. "I went in to Khadija (his wife) and said, "Cover me! Cover me!" until the terror had left me. He then came to me and said, "O Muhammad, you are the Messenger of God"" Unable to rationalize the ordeal he had just experienced, Muhammad concluded that he was possessed with an evil spirit and was thinking of committing suicide, when the mysterious figure reappeared. Presenting himself as the angel Gabriel, he told Muhammad again that he was the Messenger of God and ordered him to recite. "What shall I recite?" asked Muhammad. The angel did not reply. Instead, he caught the terrified

Meccan in a vice-like embrace until Muhammad heard God's words squeezed out of his mouth: "Recite: in the Name of thy Lord who created, created man of a blood-clot. Recite: And thy Lord is the Most Generous who taught by the Pen, taught Man that he knew not." Thus came the first in a long string of revelations, which would eventually be grouped into chapters (*suras*) of the holy book that would come to be known as the Qur'an: 'The Recitation.'[156]

This account is from Efraim Karsh, Professor of Middle East and Mediterranean Studies at King's College London, and director of the Philadelphia-based think tank the Middle East Forum, in his benchmark book, *Islamic Imperialism*. In the book, Karsh articulates the designs of Islam to global conquest, and relates historical events with current trends within Islam. As Karsh relates in his book, the angelic source of Mohammad's "recitations" led him to believe that he had been given a divine imperative to conquer the entire world and subjugate all people to Allah. Karsh writes about the rapid growth of Islamic conquests and the spread of the Islamic Caliphate into southern Europe in the 7th century, a mere one hundred years after the death of Mohammad. At the height of the Ottoman Empire, Muslims controlled a vast area that included much of Eastern Europe.

In 1682, Sultan Mehmet IV declared war on the Holy Roman Empire headquartered in Vienna. The main Ottoman army finally laid siege to Vienna on July 14, 1683. On the same day, Kara Mustafa sent the traditional demand for surrender to the city. The Viennese had demolished many of the houses around the city walls and cleared the debris, leaving an empty plain that would expose the Ottomans to defensive fire if they tried to rush the city. The fortifications of Vienna were strong and up to date, and the Ottomans had to find a more effective use for their gunpowder: mining. Archeological excavations in Vienna expose the strategy. Tunnels were dug under the massive city walls to blow them up with substantial quantities of black powder.

The King of Poland, Jan III Sobieski, prepared a relief expedition to Vienna during the summer of 1683, honoring his obligations to the treaty he had made with Leopold I, the Emperor of the Holy Roman Empire. The victory at Vienna saved Europe from Islamic conquest. The date? September 11, 1683! As a result of their defeat at Vienna, the Ottoman Empire languished until it was finally forced to relinquish its control at the end of WWI. The sultanate was abolished on November 1, 1922, and the last sultan, Mehmed VI, left the country two weeks later. The transformation to a secular governance was guaranteed when the Grand National Assembly of Turkey declared the Republic of Turkey on October 29, 1923. The caliphate was abolished on March 3, 1924.

However, even with the end of the Ottoman Caliphate, Islamic world conquest was still the aim of religious revivalists like Abul Ala Mawdudi who wrote: "The power to rule over the whole earth has been promised to the whole community of believers," This universal state, or rather world empire, was to be established through a sustained jihad that would "destroy those regimes opposed to the precepts of Islam and replace them with a government based on Islamic principles, not merely in one specific region, but [as part] of a comprehensive Islamic transformation throughout the entire world."[157]

I find it extremely interesting that President Barak Ussain Obama's first foreign excursion took him to the very place where the Islamic caliphate was abolished. He addressed the Turkish Parliament in April 2009, as the *New York Times* reported: "President Obama formally began his outreach to the Muslim world, telling legislators that the United States 'is not and will never be at war with Islam.'" But that statement denies the facts of history. On the day that United Airlines flight 175 and American

Airlines flight 11 lifted off from Boston's Logan airport, bound for a fiery collision with the twin towers of New York's World Trade Center, a lone observer watched from below. That observer was the U.S.S. Constitution, the oldest commissioned ship in the U.S. Navy and an early eyewitness to the ravages of Middle Eastern terrorism. "Old Ironsides," as she was named by her crew was built to wage war on the Muslim pirates operating along North Africa's Barbary Coast. For nearly four centuries Muslim ships prowled the Mediterranean in search of easy prey among the much slower merchant vessels of the time. In 1803, after the previous administration's appeasement policies had proven futile, newly elected President Thomas Jefferson ordered the U.S.S. Constitution to battle, and the American battle cry was, "millions for defense, but not one cent for tribute." After many successful encounters with the Muslim corsairs at sea, in 1805 the Constitution supported the landing of the U.S. Marines on "the shores of Tripoli", in an action that was immortalized in the Marine Corps hymn. That military action led ultimately to the signing aboard the deck of the Constitution of a treaty with the Muslim pasha who had declared war on the U.S. that halted raids on American shipping and the repatriation of captured American sailors.

Long before President Thomas Jefferson commissioned the USS Constitution, he dealt with Islam on the diplomatic level. Much has been made recently by revisionist historians of the fact that Thomas Jefferson owned a copy of the Quran. He wrote that one of the reasons he owned the Quran was so that he would better understand our young nation's enemies. In 1785, he and John Adams were sent to London to negotiate with the envoy from Tripoli, the representative of the Muslim pasha who had been pirating American merchant ships. Upon inquiring "concerning the ground of the pretensions to make war upon nations who had done them no injury", the ambassador replied: "It was written in their Koran, that all nations which had not acknowledged the Prophet were sinners, whom it was the right and duty of the faithful to plunder and enslave; and that every mussulman who was slain in this warfare was sure to go to paradise."[158]

Just two months after addressing the Turkish Parliament, President Obama was in Cairo where he delivered a speech titled *A New Beginning* to a receptive audience at the Major Reception Hall at Cairo University in Egypt. Egypt was chosen for Obama's speech because as then White House Press Secretary Robert Gibbs said, "It is a country that in many ways represents the heart of the Arab world." Just six months later, the string of protests, uprisings, governments overthrown, and civil war called "The Arab Spring," tracked by news media around the world, led to the declaration of a new global caliphate in a mosque in Mosul, Iraq, by Abu Bakr al-Baghdadi, the leader of the Islamic State, a man we released from Abu Grab prison where we had him in custody from 2005 to 2009. Upon his release, he told U.S. officials, "I'll see you in New York." The world watched in horror as the atrocities piled up – the beheading of American journalist James Foley and the burning alive of another Muslim, a pilot serving in the Royal Jordanian Air Force, and many more blatant acts of brutality against those Islam calls "infidels."

Lest we be deceived, let's eradicate the myths concerning Islam.

Myth #1 – "Islam is a religion of peace." Let's ask some of its most famous adherents. "I was ordered to fight all men until they say, 'There is no god but Allah.'" (Muhammad's farewell address, March 632)[159] "I shall cross this sea to their islands to pursue them until there remains no one on the face of the earth who does not acknowledge Allah." (Saladin, January 1189)[160] "We will export our revolution throughout the world ... until the calls 'there is no god but Allah and Muhammad is the messenger of Allah' are echoed all over the world" (Ayatollah Ruhollah Khomeini, 1979)[161] "I was ordered to fight the people until they say, 'There is no god but Allah and his prophet Muhammad.'" (Osama bin Laden, November 2001)[162]

Myth #2 – "Islam is a religion of love"

Search the Quran, but you will not find love. One out of seven verses are about judgment and hellfire.

Myth #3 – "Allah is the same God as the God of the Bible."

Islam may have begun with Muhammad, but its practices did not – in the days of Abraham, the primary deity of the pagan world was Al-Ilah, the moon god. Al-Ilah was the "Lord of the Kaaba," a pagan temple and its 360 idols located in Mecca. The Hajj is an annual pilgrimage to the Kaaba and marching around it seven times and then running to the Wadi Minah to throw stones at the devil all predated Muhammad – rituals kept by the Quraysh tribe of his ancestry. Pilgrims came in the hope of being granted permission to climb the steps and to kiss the black stone – a meteorite venerated in a niche in the Kaaba.

Myth #4 – "The Koran is compatible with the Bible."

Many of the stories in the Quran are merely twisted perversions of the biblical account of people, places, and events.

Myth #5 – "Islam venerates Jesus Christ."

In the Koran, Jesus is considered merely another prophet.

Islam divides the world into three houses: #1 - Dar al Islam – "The House of Islam" – Where Islam dominates. #2 - Dar al Saalem – "The House of Peace" – Where Islam accommodates the unbelievers – the dhimmis #3- Dar al Harb – "The House of War" – Where Islam wages jihad to conquer the infidels.

Islam dominates in seventy of the 184 countries in the world today. Fifty of those countries control vast wealth and resources. There are currently 1.5 billion Muslims in the world. If just ten percent of Muslims in the world today are "fundamentalists," that's 150 million people. If just ten percent of Muslim "fundamentalists" in the world today are "radical extremists," that's 15 million potential terrorists!

Muhammad's successor, Abu-Bkr said: "The only sure way in Islam of achieving paradise is to sacrifice one's life in jihad. Suicide is forbidden as self-murder; but to sacrifice one's life in killing infidels carries the highest reward."[163] Ayatollah Ruhollah Khomeini said: "The purest joy in Islam is to kill and be killed for Allah." Osama bin Laden said: "This is a war between Islam and Christianity." Islamic terrorism is just the most recent exacerbation of an ancient hatred, a theological war of supernatural origin spawned by the deceiver.

SECTION 2

DELUSION

Now that we have unmasked the deceiver and identified those who suppress the truth, and exposed how deception has infiltrated every area of our life, and investigated some of the results, let's consider the delusion that looms on the horizon. *Merriam Webster's Collegiate Dictionary* defines delusion as the act of deluding or the state of being deluded or something that is falsely or delusively believed or propagated or a persistent false psychotic belief regarding the self or persons or objects outside the self that is maintained despite indisputable evidence to the contrary; also: the abnormal state marked by such beliefs.

CHAPTER 5

UNDERTOW

In the 1970's, we lived in Seal Beach, a small town along the Coast Highway just south of Long Beach in Southern California. Our little house on 12th Street was located just a couple of houses away from the beach. On many days after work, I would park my Triumph Spitfire, run into the house, and change into my swimsuit, grab my fins, and head to the beach and the pier for some body surfing. It was a lot of fun catching waves, but I always had to be aware of the undertow. Because Seal Beach is a shore break, sometimes I just could not avoid getting caught in that powerful current that would grab me in its cold grip and take me where I did not want to go. Undertow is a subsurface flow of water returning seaward from shore as result of wave action. If there is an area under the waves where water can flow back out to sea more easily (such as a break in a sand bar) then a narrow rip current can form. A rip current is much more powerful and thus more hazardous to inexperienced people than an ordinary undertow. All around the world, lifeguards must rescue people caught in rip currents every day.

Thanks for the memories, Denny. But what does undertow and rip currents have to do with us today? Great question. The Bible warns us that there is an unprecedented undertow coming that will grab the entire world in its grip and pull them down to destruction. The apostle Paul described it in his second letter to believers in Thessalonica: "The coming of the *lawless one* is according to the working of Satan, with all power, signs, and lying wonders, and with all unrighteous deception among those who perish, because they did not receive the love of the truth, that they might be saved. And for this reason God will send them strong delusion, that they should believe the lie, that they all may be condemned who did not believe the truth but had pleasure in unrighteousness."[164] Paul warned the church that there is coming a downward spiral, a vortex, an undertow, a rip current that will begin with deception - that will develop into strong delusion - that will ultimately bring damnation. And it begins with a departure from the truth. Jesus described the sad alliance the religious leaders of His day had made with the devil because they refused to hear the truth Jesus had come to bring them: "You are of *your* father the devil, and the desires of your father you want to do. He was a murderer from the beginning, and does not stand in the truth, because there is no truth in him. When he speaks a lie, he speaks from his own *resources,* for he is a liar and the father of it."[165] The lie that the world will accept is certainly not a new one. In his letter to the Romans, Paul the apostle described the downward spiral of deception and delusion as having its origins in the willful suppression of the truth about creation and willful substitution of worship and service to the material universe over the invisible Creator. Paul identified the culprits as those "who suppress the truth in unrighteousness" and those "who exchanged the truth of God for the lie."

SCOPES TRIAL

Fostered by the abandonment of the literal interpretation of the Bible during the so-called "Age of Enlightenment" in Europe, public opinion in America was swayed by a series of events that began when the State Legislature of Tennessee passed the Butler Act on March 21, 1925. The law read: "That it shall be unlawful for any teacher in any of the Universities, Normals, and all other public schools of the State which are supported in whole or in part by the public school funds of the State, to teach any theory that denies the Story of the Divine Creation of man as taught in the Bible, and to teach instead that man has descended from a lower order of animals."[166]

At first, no one expected very much would come of the law. It was merely in the books to pacify those who interpreted the Bible literally. Within days, however, the ACLU voted to test the constitutionality of the law. John T. Scopes, a biology teacher who taught the theory of evolution, agreed to submit to arrest. Clarence Darrow, a famous criminal lawyer in his day, agreed to defend Scopes without fee. On the other side of the issue, the World's Fundamentalist Association hired the renowned William Jennings Bryan to assist the prosecution. A Christian fundamentalist and three-time nominee for President on the Democratic ticket, it was thought that William Jennings Bryan would counter the prestige of Darrow.

On July 10, 1925, the trial began in Dayton, Tennessee. To everyone's surprise, one of Darrow's first moves was to call Bryan as a witness. Here's a report of what happened:

> Darrow read from Genesis: 'And the morning and the evening were the first day.' Then he asked Bryan if he believed that the sun was created on the fourth day. Bryan said he did. 'How could there have been morning and evening without any sun?' Darrow inquired. Bryan mopped his bald dome in silence. There were snickers from the crowd, even among the faithful ... 'And you believe that God punished the serpent by condemning snakes

forever after to crawl upon their bellies?' 'I believe that!' Bryan retorted. 'Well, have you any idea how the snake went before that?' The crowd laughed, and Bryan turned livid. His voice rose and the fan in his hand shook in anger. 'Your honor,' he said, 'I will answer all Mr. Darrow's questions at once. I want the world to know that this man who does not believe in God is using a Tennessee court to cast slurs on Him.' 'I object to that statement,' Darrow shouted. 'I am examining you on your fool ideas that no intelligent Christian on earth believes.'[167]

The result of the outcome of the trial, consequently, has been that the theory of evolution has long been the required teaching of public education and has been force fed to students as the facts of science and nature. Though it cannot be proven by available data and has never been observed to occur, evolution is nevertheless considered fact by most Americans. Sadly, surveys indicate that 70% of people in America who identify themselves as Christians also believe in evolution.

HERE COME THE ALIENS

What follows is the expectation that if life evolved on earth by chance, then it could have developed similarly on other planets as well. Moreover, such beings might possess science and technology far beyond mankind's capabilities. The possibility that we are not alone in the universe is extremely exciting to most people and has been the popular subject of books, articles, television, and movies for many years. It is not just pop culture that speculates what might happen when extraterrestrial beings are first discovered. Serious international efforts have been underway for years to contact extraterrestrials. In the US, the program is titled SETI – Search for Extraterrestrial Intelligence. Vast amounts of taxpayer's money are poured into this and other efforts. These efforts have been fueled by the belief that alien beings exist and that it is only a matter of time until we make contact. But a more important question is: Will that contact be with benevolent, kind beings as portrayed in movies like *Close Encounters of the Third Kind, E.T. the Extraterrestrial,* or *Contact* – or will that first encounter be with cruel, warlike creatures as portrayed in *Independence Day, War of the Worlds,* or *Mars Attacks*? What if the extraterrestrials were not inhabitants of some distant planet, but were, in fact, spirit beings fallen from heaven doing the bidding of Satan? They might appear as "angels of light," bringing a joyful response from humanity; and no wonder, for Satan himself transforms himself into an angel of light.[168] Far-fetched, you say. Robert Jastrow, founder and for many years the director of the Goddard Institute for Space Studies, suggested that life beyond earth may be: "far beyond the flesh-and-blood form that we would recognize. It may (have) … escaped its mortal flesh to become something that old-fashioned people would call spirits. And so how do we know it's there? Maybe it can materialize and then dematerialize. I'm sure it has magical powers by our standards."

The idea that aliens operating spacecraft might be other than extraterrestrials is being supported by some researchers into the UFO phenomenon, as well. Jacques Vallee, an astrophysicist, and computer scientist, one of the world's most credible UFO researchers, wrote in his book *Dimensions: A Casebook of Alien Contact* that "some witnesses have thought that they had seen demons." and goes on to speculate that the UFO phenomenon may well be the strategy of spirit beings, not aliens.

Whitley Strieber, author of *Communion* and *Transformation,* described his own encounter with an alien creature:

> Increasingly I felt as if I were entering a struggle
> for my soul, my essence, or whatever part of me

might have reference to the eternal. There were worse things than death, I suspected. And I was beginning to get the distinct impression that one of them had taken an interest in me. So far the word demon had never been spoken among the scientists and doctors who were working with me. And why should it have been? We were beyond such things. We were a group of atheists and agnostics, far too sophisticated to be concerned with such archaic ideas as demons and angels. I felt an absolutely indescribable sense of menace … and yet I couldn't move, couldn't cry out and couldn't get away. I lay as still as death, suffering inner agonies. Whatever was there seemed so monstrously ugly, so filthy and dark and sinister. Of course they were demons. They had to be. And they were here and I couldn't get away. I couldn't save my poor family. I still remember that thing crouching there, so terribly ugly, its arms and legs like the limbs of a great insect, its eyes glaring at me.

MERCURY THEATER

The headlines blazed across the front pages of newspapers on October 31, 1938: "Radio Fake Scares Nation." The night before, thousands of people, believing they were under attack by Martians, flooded newspaper offices and radio and police stations with calls, asking how to flee their city or how they should protect themselves from "gas raids." Scores of adults required medical treatment for shock and hysteria. What radio listeners heard that night was an adaptation, by Orson Welles' Mercury Theater group, of a science fiction novel written forty years earlier: *The War of the Worlds,* by H.G. Wells. However, the radio play, narrated by Orson Welles, had been written and performed to sound like a real news broadcast about an invasion from Mars. The hoax worked, historians say, because the broadcast authentically simulated how radio worked in an emergency. And many people held the view that an invasion from Mars was not beyond possibility.

A former director of NASA, Dr. James C. Fletcher, said, "The discovery of extraterrestrial life would eclipse all previous discoveries of mankind."[169] Roberto Pinotti, a sociologist from Florence, Italy had this to say: "The news of the existence of extraterrestrial intelligence would be devastating. It will affect every field of human activity. Contact with superior beings would be shattering."[170] As the *Los Angeles Times* wrote: "The discovery of life elsewhere could cause many earthlings to panic, and even the superpowers might find themselves inferior to the newly discovered society, and thus subject to internal instability. If there is a single consensus among those involved in the search (for extraterrestrials), it is that success would change the world forever, and that the first few days would be sheer madness."[171] Just the kind of scenario it would take to set the stage for a radical new world order – politically, religiously, and economically.

ISRAEL'S EXAMPLE

The Bible clearly states that delusion is a byproduct of forsaking God, as recorded for us in the ancient Hebrew prophecies. God spoke to Isaiah[172] and declared that he would choose the delusions that would grip the children of Israel in a perpetual state of deception as His response to their lack of repentance and obedience to His word. His indictment of the children of Israel was quite specific – First, He said: "when I called, no one answered." God continuously called out to the children of Israel, but no one answered. In other words, no one responded to God's call to action. There was no positive response – no one stepped up to the plate. Secondly, God said: "when I spoke, they did not hear." Throughout their history, God sent holy prophets to the children of Israel, but no one listened to them. God even blew the trumpet to alarm the people, but the people did not listen nor heed the warnings. God's indictment continued: "they did evil before My eyes," The people of God knew that God was constantly watching them, monitoring their conduct, but that did not stop them from doing evil right in front of Him. Lastly, God indicted the children of Israel because: "they chose that in which I do not delight." In response, God sent delusion upon them that led to their destruction, the sad result of the children of Israel's refusal to listen and respond to God's voice.

THE CHURCH IN AMERICA

But, Denny, that was then, this is now – what does that have to do with us today? Great question. The Hebrew prophet Amos was told: "'Behold, the days are coming,' says the Lord God, 'that I will send a famine on the land, not a famine of bread, nor a thirst for water, but of hearing the words of the Lord. They shall wander from sea to sea, and from north to east; they shall run to and fro, seeking the word of the Lord, but shall not find it.'"[173] God declared that this famine for the hearing of the words of the Lord would be part and parcel of the apostasy in the last days. But, Denny, what is so important about the Word of God? King David wrote the perfect reason why the Word of God is essential to us: "Your word *is* a lamp to my feet and a light to my path."[174] God's word illuminates – it shows us how well we are walking, and it illuminates the path that we are traveling. Without the Word of God, we are absolutely lost. The church in America is being turned upside down. It has forsaken God's Word and is suffering the same consequences that the children of Israel suffered so long ago. In these last days, deception is everywhere, and it is essential that Christians distinguish the difference between what is true and what is false – what is right and what is wrong.

CONFUSION

Today, people who claim to be Christians are abandoning the clear teachings of the Bible and publishing all kinds of books, like Matthew Vines' book published in 2015, *God and the Gay Christian – The Biblical Case in Support of Same-Sex Relationships.* Andrew T. Walker, an analyst for The Heritage Foundation, wrote this review: "This book need not be one hundred percent compelling or accurate in order to succeed. All that needs to happen for Vines to claim victory is for his readers to be *confused* and not necessarily *convinced* of his argument," Remember, confusion is the arena in which the deceivers operate.

Confusion is also a byproduct of forsaking God, as seen in Moses' proclamation to the children of Israel as he prophesied concerning the consequences: "The Lord will send on you cursing, confusion, and rebuke in all that you set your hand to do, until you are destroyed and until you perish quickly, because of the wickedness of your doings in which you have forsaken Me. The Lord will strike you with madness and blindness and confusion of heart. And you shall grope at noonday, as a blind man gropes in darkness;"[175] This prophesy was not aimed at a godless culture, but at the very chosen people of God. Confusion is a byproduct of the forsaking of God – no wonder the church seems confused. And those who attend some of the churches in America are like lemmings – entering those doors can be perilous. And it all begins with a departure from the truth.

APOSTASY

The similarities to what Paul wrote nearly 2,000 years ago between what God said to Isaiah nearly 2,500 years ago are unmistakable–if you do not receive the love of the truth nor believe the truth you will be subjected to strong delusion. Have you seen this headline: *Newsboys Co-founder Denounces Christianity: 'I'm Now an Atheist'*:

> The Newsboys is one of the most popular Christian bands ever—most recently reminding fans why with the hit theme song for the movie *God's Not Dead* that tackles atheism head on. That's one more reason why it's so disturbing that one of its co-founders, George Perdikis, has renounced Christ and embraced a godless worldview. "I always felt uncomfortable with the strict rules imposed by Christianity. All I wanted to do was create and play rock and roll … and yet most of the attention I received was focused on how well I maintained the impossible standards of religion. I wanted my life to be measured by my music, not by my ability to resist temptation." Perdikis left The Newsboys in 1990, which is when his heart began to stray from Christianity. In the post, he explains how he carved out a life for himself away from church and started his own "voyage of inquiry" into what he believed. He explored cosmology and was fascinated by the works of Carl Sagan, Neil deGrasse Tyson, Lawrence Krauss, Brian Cox, and Richard Dawkins. "By 2007, I renounced Christianity once and for all and declared myself an atheist," Perdikis says. Perdikis is not the first high-profile Christian rocker to reject Christ. Heavy metal Christian rock star Tim Lambesis

last June told the world he's an atheist. Not only that, he told the *Alternative Press* he figures only one in ten Christian bands he toured with were actually Christians.[176]

British songwriter and worship leader, Vicky Beeching, shocked the world when she announced that she was a lesbian. "What Jesus taught was a radical message of welcome and inclusion and love. I feel certain God loves me just the way I am, and I have a huge sense of calling to communicate that to young people,"[177] she said.

In another article published in January 2015, *Charisma News* asked: *Why Are So Many Christians Turning Into Atheists?* Here is an excerpt:

> Pastor Ryan Bell made a strange New Year's resolution in 2014—he aimed to live a godless year. Bell, no relation to universalist Rob Bell, kept a blog to chronicle his yearlong journey without God and even had a documentary crew on hand to film what turned out to be his transformation from a Seventh-Day Adventist pastor to a full-blown atheist. "I've looked at the majority of the arguments that I've been able to find for the existence of God, and on the question of God's existence or not, I have to say I don't find there to be a convincing case, in my view," Bell told NPR's Arun Rath.[178]

What? How do you move from accepting a call of God into full-time ministry only to turn your back on him and decide to exchange a close relationship with God to a 'closer relationship with reality'? The Clergy Project, a secret initiative that's willing to foot the bill to get you out of your pulpit and into a new career, claims to offer a "safe haven for active and former professional clergy/religious leaders who do not hold supernatural beliefs." What is going on? Is the church doing something wrong? Or is the culture wooing once-saved Christians to the godless side? Or both? What, then, is the root of Christians turning their back on God? Jesus said that in the last days, the love of many would grow cold because iniquity will abound.[179] When a God-fearing pastor becomes a godless champion for faithlessness, love has grown cold. Yes, Jesus said that the love of many will grow cold, but Paul the apostle warned Timothy that their conscience would be seared with a hot iron: "Now the Spirit expressly says that in latter times some will depart from the faith, giving heed to deceiving spirits and doctrines of demons, speaking lies in hypocrisy, having their own conscience seared with a hot iron"[180] Cold hearts and seared minds, so God sends delusion upon them. And remember that delusion is a persistent false psychotic belief regarding the self or persons or objects outside the self that is maintained despite indisputable evidence to the contrary; also, the abnormal state marked by such beliefs.

CHAPTER 6

THE WOMAN WHO RIDES THE BEAST

SHOW AND TELL

ONE OF MY FAVORITE ACTIVITIES in grammar school was "show & tell." Did you ever have the opportunity? The scary idea of getting in front of your classmates may have intimidated you, but it was certainly good training for your future. So, Denny, what does "show & tell" have to do with the Bible? Great question. In the Book of Revelation, the apostle John experienced show and tell. During his incredible vision about the future, an angel spoke to John and said: "Come, I will *show* you the judgment of the great harlot, I will *tell* you the mystery of the woman and of the beast that carries her,"[181] Thus, John experienced "show & tell" as the angel exposed the mystery of the woman who rides the beast.

This mysterious woman who is riding the beast is called "the great harlot." The Greek word translated "harlot" here is porne – a word derivative of our English word *pornography*. Thus, John was told about one of the aspects of this mysterious woman: she wields universal power via spiritual adultery or idolatry, confusing her followers by mixing the genuine with the false. In the Bible, the true church is called a "chaste virgin" – the apostate church is a prostitute.

Also, John was told other aspects of this mysterious woman. Her unique position is political adultery, exercising authority by controlling and governing in arenas far beyond the church. Her unlimited prosperity and unholy passion are the result of economic adultery, consuming and acquiring instead of contributing and assisting. The true church offers the cup of salvation – the apostate church holds the golden cup full of abominations. Her unsettling persecution of the saints is the result of her religious adultery, condemning and killing those who genuinely believe in Jesus Christ. The true church is purchased by the blood of Christ and drinks the cup of communion to commemorate Him – the apostate church is drunk with the blood of the martyrs of Jesus.

THE MYSTERY OF THE MOTHER

Let's consider what John saw written on her forehead: "And on her forehead a name *was* written: MYSTERY, BABYLON THE GREAT, THE MOTHER OF HARLOTS AND OF THE ABOMINATIONS OF THE EARTH."[182] She is a mystery, and she is a mother.

In Genesis, we are introduced to a man who may hold the key to understanding this mysterious woman who rides the beast. He was a master of imitation – using bricks for stone, and a master of substitution – using slime for mortar. "Cush begot Nimrod; he began to be a mighty one on the earth. He was a mighty hunter before the Lord; therefore it is said, 'Like Nimrod the mighty hunter before the Lord.' And the beginning of his kingdom was Babel, Erech, Accad, and Calneh, in the land of Shinar."[183] Let's overlay this account of Nimrod onto our text in Revelation. According to legend, after marrying a woman named Semiramis, Nimrod was killed by a wild boar while hunting. Semiramis mourned the death of her husband for forty days, after which time she discovered that she was pregnant and claimed the father was Nimrod. To commemorate this "miraculous" event, Semiramis used a golden egg. Others followed suit, coloring eggs for the celebration. She named her son Tammuz, which means "sprout of life" and declared that he was the reincarnation of Nimrod. When Tammuz died one winter day and was 'resurrected' three days later, the worshippers commemorated his death by burning a "log of the son," or "yule log." They celebrated the reappearance of Tammuz with an evergreen tree – illustrating that the log that was burned was brought back to life. Thus, each spring, people colored eggs in honor of the 'miraculous' conception of Tammuz, and decorated evergreen trees with silver and gold each winter in honor of his 'resurrection' from the dead. Now you know the pagan origins of many of the traditional celebrations at Christmastime and Easter. The sign of the cross was sacred to Tammuz, and the first letter of his name, the tau, became the symbol in Babylon for Tammuz worship. It is represented on vast numbers of the most ancient altars and temples, and did not, as many suppose, originate with Christianity.

The Lord revealed to His prophet, Jeremiah, how the children of Israel had provoked Him by their worship of this mysterious woman: "The children gather wood, the fathers kindle the fire, and the women knead dough, to make cakes for the queen of heaven; and *they* pour out drink offerings to other gods, that they may provoke Me to anger."[184] "Thus says the Lord of hosts, the God of Israel, saying: 'You and your wives have spoken with your mouths and fulfilled with your hands, saying, 'We will surely keep our vows that we have made, to burn incense to the queen of heaven and pour out drink offerings to her.'"[185] The Lord revealed how the worship of the queen of heaven had affected the women living around Jerusalem when the prophet Ezekiel was taken to the Temple: "So He brought me to the door of the north gate of the Lord's house; and to my dismay, women were sitting there weeping for Tammuz." [186]

The worship of the queen of heaven was not limited to Babylon. In Egypt, Semiramis and Tammuz became known as Isis and Horus and the ankh became the symbol in Egypt for the worship of Horus. In Canaan, they were known as Astarte (Ashtoreth) and Baal as seen in ancient statuary and manmade idols. When the children of Israel occupied Canaan, they were polluted by Baal worship. The Phoenician princess, Jezebel, championed Baal, until the prophet Elijah confronted the prophets of Baal at Mount Carmel. In Greece, Semiramis and Tammuz were known as Aphrodite and Eros. In Rome, they were known as Venus and Cupid as depicted in multitudes of sculpture and paintings. Obviously, this is an attempt to counterfeit and confuse the genuine mother and child, Mary and Jesus. It was one of the reasons that the Roman Catholic church was vulnerable – as the myths about the mystery of Semiramis and Tammuz were incorporated into the deification and worship of Mary. According to the book, *The Two Babylons*, throughout pagan religious history, there was usually a priestly order that encouraged the worship of the mother and child, practiced the sprinkling of holy water, and established an order of virgins dedicated to the gods and commanded worshippers to mourn for forty days prior to the great festival of Ishtar in remembrance of the death of Nimrod. When the Babylonian cult eventually made its way to Pergamos, the chief priests wore crowns in the form of a fish, in recognition of Dagon, the fish god, with the title *Keeper of the Bridge*. The Latin equivalent is *Pontifex Maximus*, first used by the Caesars and later the Emperors of Rome, and ultimately by the Pope, the Bishop of Rome.

THE BASKET OF LEAVEN

Jesus told His disciples a parable that we should consider carefully: "Another parable He spoke to them: 'The kingdom of heaven is like leaven, which a woman took and hid in three measures of meal till it was all leavened.'"[187] In the Bible, leaven is always a symbol of evil, a symbol of corruption. Thus, Jesus was telling His disciples about the evil pollution that a woman would introduce into the kingdom of heaven until it was totally corrupted. Perhaps Jesus was referring to an ancient prophecy:

> Then the angel who talked with me came out and said to me, "Lift your eyes now, and see what this *is* that goes forth." So I asked, "What *is* it?" And he said, "It *is* a basket that is going forth." He also said, "This *is* their resemblance throughout the earth: Here *is* a lead disc lifted up, and this *is* a woman sitting inside the basket;" then he said, "This *is* Wickedness!" And he thrust her down into the basket, and threw the lead cover over its mouth. Then I raised my eyes and looked, and there *were* two women, coming with the wind in their wings; for they had wings like the wings of a stork, and they lifted up the basket between earth and heaven. So I said to the angel who talked with me, "Where are they carrying the basket?" And he said to me, "To build a house for it in the land of Shinar; when it is ready, *the basket* will be set there on its base."[188]

In the parable we read, where did the woman hide the leaven? That's right. In three measures of meal. The word *measure* in this passage refers to a Hebrew unit of dry measure called a seah. What I find extremely interesting is the fact that we know three seahs = one ephah. And the English word for the Hebrew word *ephah* is bushel or basket. The woman hid the leaven in three measures of meal – or in one basket. Which makes our understanding of the repeated use of *basket* in the prophecy of Zechariah more complete. And where exactly will the house be built where the basket will be established? In the land of Shinar – as every student of the Bible knows, the land of Shinar is another name for what? That's right. Babylon. The woman is hidden inside the basket with the lead lid on until the appropriate time for its establishment in Shinar.

THE APPARITIONS

Now let's turn our attention to another aspect of this prophecy. Now, things get current. *Resemblance* here is the English translation of the Hebrew word *ayin*, which means eye, or appearance. It is a fact of modern history that there have been lots of *appearances*. I have visited the Basilica de Guadalupe in Mexico City, where millions of pilgrims come each year to see Our Lady of Guadalupe, the image of Mary reportedly divinely imprinted upon the cloak of Juan Diego, a Catholic priest in Mexico in 1531. Perhaps the most famous and popular apparition of Mary occurred in Fatima, Portugal, when on May 13, 1917, Lucia Santos and her two cousins say Mary appeared to them. Then, on October 13, 1917, thousands of people say they witnessed "the miracle of the Sun," an interesting connection to the "lead disc lifted up" in the prophecy of Zechariah. In addition to the millions of pilgrims who come each year to worship Mary and to pray to her at the Sanctuary of Our Lady of Fatima, Popes have knelt before her statue.

In cover article after cover article in popular publications like *Life*, *Newsweek*, and *Time* magazines writers ask: "Why are 2 billion Hail Marys said daily? Why did 5 million people, many non-Christian, visit Lourdes this year to drink the healing waters? Why did more than 10 million trek to Guadalupe to pray to Our Lady? Why the apparitions? Why are Mary hymns creeping into Methodist songbooks? What is it about Mary? One of the most intriguing aspects of the latest rise of Mary is this: The emotional need for her is so irresistible to a troubled world that people without an obvious link to the Virgin are being drawn to her. It's not news that Muslims revere Mary as a pure and holy saint – she's mentioned thirty-four times in the Quran ... but to see large numbers of Muslims making pilgrimages to Christian Marian shrines is a remarkable thing."

THE QUEEN OF HEAVEN

But it is not only religious people who are drawn to these appearances. As David Leeming and Jake Page wrote in *Goddess-Myths of the Female Divine*:

> But Goddess has never died, and one of the major spiritual and psychological phenomena of our time has been her reemergence as a significant prescience in our lives. She has founded a central place in several of the great world religions – particularly, Catholicism and Hinduism. Goddess has been revived in modern cults, the spiritual ancestors of which are the earth cults of Demeter, Isis, and Asherah. She has made herself known in the metaphors, the myths, of modern science – particularly, psychology and climatology. She has expressed herself politically and sociologically in the drive for a new wholeness – a new spiritual, psychological, and physical ecology – that is the power behind what we call the women's movement. Goddess is returning because she is needed. The return of Goddess in the patriarchal religious context is most clearly illustrated in the progress of the Virgin Mary from her original status in the New Testament as humble birth-giver and

grieving mother to that of immaculately conceived
Queen of Heaven.[189]

And indeed, the queen of heaven is showing up everywhere –
on the coffee cup from Starbucks which you are drinking - floating
on a barge on the Willamette River carried by flatbed truck
through city streets to be enshrined on October 6, 1985 in front
of the Portland Building in downtown Portland, Oregon to
commemorate the Seal of the City of Portland. Thanks to our
study of the Bible and the promise that Jesus made to His disciples
that the Holy Spirit would lead us into all truth and reveal the
future, we now know that the so-called queen of heaven is an
ancient false religious system – The Woman Who Rides the
Beast, a spiritual prostitute.

AN EVIL SEDUCTRESS

Sometimes things that are evil are both fascinating and repugnant.
When the apostle John saw the woman riding the beast, he found
her both riveting and revolting. He could not take his eyes off the
woman who epitomized evil throughout human history. She was
opulently clothed in jewels and robes of royalty. The cup she held
in her hand was pure gold on the outside but filled with putrid
potions. She was intoxicated, but not by alcohol, but by the blood
of true believers. And the beast she was riding on was a terrible and
terrifying creature. It had seven heads and ten horns. It was covered
by blasphemous graffiti, and it was scarlet, the color of spilled
blood. As John watched and wondered, an angel came to show
and tell him the mystery of the woman and the beast upon whom
she was seated. The angel exposed just how gross this woman is
really. All the kings of the earth have committed adultery with her,
and she is so universally immoral that her conduct has intoxicated
most people on the earth. She is exposed as an evil seductress.

When God's prophet Nahum pronounced judgment on the great ancient City of Nineveh, he used the same paradigm: "Because of the multitude of harlotries of the seductive harlot, the mistress of sorceries, who sells nations through her harlotries, and families through her sorceries."[190] James, the half-brother of Jesus, used that same paradigm when he warned: "Adulterers and adulteresses! Do you not know that friendship with the world is enmity with God? Whoever therefore wants to be a friend of the world makes himself an enemy of God."[191] The world, as James saw it, was the secular system that excludes God and is under Satan's control.

AN ANGELIC WARNING

The Woman Who Rides the Beast symbolizes a global false religious system that is so appealing that she has been able to seduce all the kings of the earth with her deceptions and intoxicate entire populations. What kind of religious system will appeal to such a diverse world? What secret will lie behind her ability to bring into submission an atheist, a Buddhist, a Muslim, a Hindu, a professing Christian? The universal appeal and the cunning, deceptive nature of this false religious system will become part of the delusion that God will send upon on those who reject the truth. May the warning given by an angel to John be taken seriously: "And I heard another voice from heaven saying, 'Come out of her, my people, lest you share in her sins, and lest you receive of her plagues. For her sins have reached to heaven, and God has remembered her iniquities."[192]

THE MYSTERY OF THE BEAST

His enemies reject it, and His friends neglect it. Few take the time to read it. Of course, I am talking about the Book of Revelation, known originally by its title in Greek: *Apokalypsis*. The unveiling – not a coverup, but the uncovering of the mystery of the ages – Jesus Christ. A lifting of a curtain to show us what can no longer be concealed – the Person, Plan, Power, and Purpose of Jesus Christ in His glory. In the first part of chapter seven John was shown the judgment of the woman who "rides" the beast – then he was told the mystery of the beast that "carries" her: "But the angel said to me, 'Why did you marvel? I will tell you the mystery of the woman and of the beast that carries her, which has the seven heads and the ten horns. The beast that you saw was, and is not, and will ascend out of the bottomless pit and go to perdition.'"[193] Thus, John was reminded about the origin and destiny of the beast – his satanic, demonic origin from the abyss and his ultimate judgment and sentence – "perdition" – utter destruction. The angel continued:

> And those who dwell on the earth will marvel, whose names are not written in the Book of Life from the foundation of the world, when they see the beast that was, and is not, and yet is. Here *is* the mind which has wisdom: The seven heads are seven mountains on which the woman sits. There are also seven kings. Five have fallen, one is, *and* the other has not yet come. And when he comes, he must continue a short time. The beast that was, and is not, is himself also the eighth, and is of the seven, and is going to perdition. The ten horns which you saw are ten kings who have received no kingdom as yet, but they receive authority for one hour as kings with the beast.[194]

King David provided a clue that may help us uncover the details of this mystery: "Lord, by Your favor You have made my mountain stand strong;"[195] David, of course, used *my mountain* as a description of his kingdom and his reign. Daniel employed the same imagery when he described the kingdom of Jesus Christ and His reign on earth: "And the stone that struck the image became a great mountain and filled the whole earth."[196]

THE PARADE OF WORLD EMPIRES

Let's consider the significance of Daniel's interpretation of King Nebuchadnezzar's dream and the statue Nebuchadnezzar saw. The head of gold represented the Babylonian Empire (606 B.C. – 539 B.C.); the chest and arms of silver represented the Medo-Persian Empire (539 B.C. – 331 B.C.); the belly of brass represented the Grecian Empire (331 B.C. – 133 B.C.); the legs of iron represented the two divisions of the Roman Empire (Western - 133 B.C. – 476 A.D. – Eastern - 133 B.C. – 1453 A.D); the feet of iron mixed with clay represented the Revived Roman Empire that is not yet revealed in the world today. Thus, the Lord revealed to King Nebuchadnezzar, through Daniel's interpretation of his dream, the succession of world empires from Babylon until the last world empire – the Revived Roman Empire. But the meaning of the seven kings in Revelation 17 begins not with Babylon, but with the first world empire Assyria, followed by the Egyptian Empire. Both preceded Babylon. John was told by the angel that "five have fallen" – Assyria, Egypt, Babylon, Medo-Persia, and Greece. John was told by the angel that "one is." Rome was the empire that ruled the world when John heard the words spoken by the angel. However, the angel also said, "the other has not yet come." So, Denny, when will the Roman Empire be revived? Great question. Let me try to explain.

THE REVIVED ROMAN EMPIRE

Out from the devastation of the bombing of Britain, London suffered the Nazi blitzkrieg causing huge fires in the bombing's aftermath and leaving men, women, and children to contend with drastic, difficult days which brought about the Allied Forces response and an aerial bombing campaign aimed at the destruction of the Nazis' industrial and military might, igniting oil refineries and destroying their factories which ultimately led to the Allied victory in Europe.

After the end of the Second World War, in his speech delivered on September 19, 1946, at the University of Zürich, Switzerland, Winston Churchill concluded that: "We must build a kind of United States of Europe. In this way only will hundreds of millions of toilers be able to regain the simple joys and hopes which make life worth living. The process is simple. All that is needed is the resolve of hundreds of millions of men and women to do right instead of wrong and to gain as their reward blessing instead of cursing."[197] His perspective resonated with most of Europe, and the Treaty of Paris in 1951 formed the European Coal and Steel Community. The Treaty of Rome in 1958 formed the European Economic Community. The Maastricht Treaty (formally, the Treaty on European Union or TEU) was signed on February 7, 1992, by the members of the European Community in Maastricht, Netherlands. It created the European Union and led to the creation of the single European currency, the euro. The treaty of Lisbon signed in 2009 has brought the EU to where it is today with twenty-seven nations in full membership.

Look at coins minted by the EU, and you will see engraved the image adopted by that government as a permanent symbol – a woman riding a beast. A metal statue of a woman riding the beast stands just outside the entrance of the headquarters of the European Union in Brussels, Belgium. Seen from any angle, the symbol is revealing. In addition, the EU decided to use the painting of the Tower of Babel – painted by Peter Brueghel in the 16th Century as the template for the design of their building where their Parliament meets. They have printed and distributed posters based on that painting with the banner: *Europe – Many*

Tongues – One Voice. The angel informed john: "These are of one mind, and they will give their power and authority to the beast."[198]

THE COMING WORLD LEADER

Belgium's Premier, Paul Henri Spaak – First President of the United Nations General Assembly and a key planner in the formation of the European Economic Community in 1957, whose image was pictured on the May 10, 1948, issue of *TIME* magazine said: "We do not want another committee; we have too many already. What we want is a man of sufficient stature to hold the allegiance of all the people and to lift us up out of the economic morass into which we are sinking. Send us such a man, and whether he be God or devil, we will receive him."[199] Noted British historian Arnold Toynbee said: "The nations are ready to give the kingdoms of the world to any one man who will offer us a solution to our world's problems."[200]

On July 24, 2008, a crowd estimated at 200,000 flooded the streets of Berlin to hear a speech delivered by a United States Senator campaigning for US President. The enthusiastic crowd not only welcomed him but held high hopes that he would be the leader for which the world was then and is now so desperate. After Barack Obama was elected President – Henry Kissinger seized on that enthusiasm and wrote an op-ed piece for the International Herald Tribune titled *The Chance for a New World Order:* "The extraordinary impact of the president-elect on the imagination of humanity is an important element in shaping a new world order."[201] That phrase, 'new world order' traces back at least as far as 1940, when author H. G. Wells used it as a title for his book about a socialist, unified, one-world government. The book was republished in 2007.

The world has a dream and is ready to deify anyone who can deliver on that dream. Despite the impact on the imagination of humanity, Barack Obama returned to Berlin as President of the United States and gave another speech, this time at the Brandenburg Gate on June 13, 2013, and only 4,500 people showed up. The contrast in turnout is stunning but indicates that the world is hungry for a leader who will deliver on his promises. The problems the world faces are gloomy, global, and growing: global terrorism, the continuing global economic crisis and the powerlessness of the current world leaders to solve the problems; the war in Gaza; the war in Ukraine; the military buildup in China; the threat of nuclear missiles launched from North Korea who have been helping the development of Iran's missile program amid their efforts to acquire nuclear weapons and their ongoing threats to wipe Israel off the map, and to ultimately destroy America, whom they describe as the "Great Satan." And back here at home we are bombarded every day with more unwelcome news.

The identity of the coming world leader is hidden and will not be revealed until the presence of the Holy Spirit in the church has been removed as the apostle Paul told the believers in Thessalonica:

> Let no one deceive you by any means; for *that Day will not come* unless the falling away comes first, and the man of sin is revealed, the son of perdition, who opposes and exalts himself above all that is called God or that is worshiped, so that he sits as God in the temple of God, showing himself that he is God. Do you not remember that when I was still with you I told you these things? And now you know what is restraining, that he may be revealed in his own time. For the mystery of lawlessness is already at work; only He who now restrains *will do so* until He is taken out of the way and then the lawless one will be revealed.[202]

JUSTICE TO THE APOSTATE CHURCH

In God's economy, He will use the coming world leader, "the lawless one", "the beast" and those who support him to administer justice to the apostate church: "Then he said to me, 'The waters which you saw, where the harlot sits, are peoples, multitudes, nations, and tongues. And the ten horns which you saw on the beast, these will hate the harlot, make her desolate and naked, eat her flesh and burn her with fire. For God has put it into their hearts to fulfill His purpose, to be of one mind, and to give their kingdom to the beast, until the words of God are fulfilled.'"[203]

Isn't it fitting that the ultimate destruction of the apostate world religious system is not at all unlike the burning at the stake of Christian martyrs in Europe - like William Tyndale who translated the Greek manuscripts of the Bible into English. Tyndale's final words, spoken before he was strangled to death and then burned at the stake were: "Lord! Open the King of England's eyes." Like Joan of Arc, arrested, tried, and condemned by the church and burned at the stake for heresy.

And now you know the mystery of the woman who rides the beast.

SECTION 3

DELIVERANCE

But before it is too late, we need to remember that there is deliverance. God promised to deliver anyone who is willing to listen when He speaks and to answer when He calls. First, we discovered deception is rampant everywhere. Second, we dealt with delusion – the perpetual state of deception - and now, let's dive into deliverance.

CHAPTER 7

PENTECOST

WHEN THE CHILDREN OF ISRAEL were delivered from their bitter bondage in Egypt, God's presence dwelt in the tabernacle and His presence there was signified by the pillar of fire that stood above the tabernacle. 1,500 years later, Jesus came to the Temple in Jerusalem and taught. He presented Himself to Israel with all the credentials of their promised Messiah. But His own people, the children of Israel, rejected Him, and He lamented, "O Jerusalem, Jerusalem, the one who kills the prophets and stones those who are sent to her! How often I wanted to gather your children together, as a hen *gathers* her brood under *her* wings, but you were not willing! See! Your house is left to you desolate; and assuredly, I say to you, you shall not see Me until *the time* comes when you say, 'Blessed is He who comes in the name of the LORD!'"[204] After the nation rejected Him, He went to the Cross to die for our sins. He was buried in a borrowed tomb, but the grave could not hold Him – on the third day He rose from among the dead. Hallelujah! He is Risen! God has always had a wonderful plan.

Despite Israel's rejection of the Messiah, on the Day of Pentecost, fifty days after Jesus was crucified on Passover, the Holy Spirit was poured out upon the 120 disciples gathered in the upper room in Jerusalem. The physical evidence of the event was the sound of a rushing mighty wind and what appeared to be flame above the head of each of them. Now, remember, these disciples were Jews who would have been reminded of the "pillar of fire" that resided above the tabernacle in the center of their ancestors' encampments as they were lead on their journey from bitter bondage in Egypt to the land of promise. As they looked around the room at one another, I believe that they recognized the flame above each head as the Lord filled them with the Holy Spirit on that day as the sign that their body then became the temple of the living God.

As a crowd of over 3,000 people gathered to see what was happening to the disciples on that day of Pentecost nearly 2,000 years ago, Peter clearly explained what the outpouring of the Holy Spirit meant for God's plan of deliverance. Inspired by the Holy Spirit, Peter turned the attention of everyone present that day to the words written by the prophet Joel and declared that what those disciples were experiencing was the fulfillment of that prophecy. Let's read exactly what he said:

> But this is what was spoken by the prophet Joel: "And it shall come to pass in the last days, says God, 'that I will pour out of My Spirit on all flesh; your sons and your daughters shall prophesy, your young men shall see visions, your old men shall dream dreams. And on My menservants and on My maidservants I will pour out My Spirit in those days; and they shall prophesy. I will show wonders in heaven above and signs in the earth beneath: blood and fire and vapor of smoke. The sun shall be turned into darkness, and the moon into blood, before the coming of the great and awesome day of the Lord. And it shall come to pass that whoever calls on the name of the Lord shall be saved.'[205]

In the prophecy of Joel that Peter quoted, God spoke regarding three things that He would do in the last days – beginning with the outpouring of the Holy Spirit. Secondly, God spoke and said: "I will show wonders in heaven above and signs in the earth beneath" - and thirdly: "And it shall come to pass that whoever calls on the name of the Lord shall be saved." So, let's turn our attention one by one to these important aspects of God's plan.

THE MINISTRY OF THE HOLY SPIRIT

First, let's consider the current ministry of the Holy Spirit. On the night He was betrayed, Jesus prepared His disciples for their future after His ascension and identified the person and program of the Holy Spirit: "And I will pray the Father, and He will give you another Helper, that He may abide with you forever—the Spirit of truth, whom the world cannot receive, because it neither sees Him nor knows Him; but you know Him, for He dwells with you and will be in you."[206] Jesus promised that the Holy Spirit would be an invisible influence in the world and in the life of every believer.

Jesus also described the current ministry of the Holy Spirit in the world to unbelievers: "And when He has come, He will convict the world of sin, and of righteousness, and of judgment:"[207] What did Jesus mean? When we read the word, "convict" we immediately think of someone who has been arrested, tried, and convicted of a crime. However, Jesus used the word in the sense of the Holy Spirit convincing people about God's perspective concerning sin, righteousness, and judgment. Jesus amplified what He meant: "of sin, because they do not believe in Me; of righteousness, because I go to My Father and you see Me no more; of judgment, because the ruler of this world is judged."[208]

When you think of the word, *sin*, what comes to mind? Lying, cheating, stealing, adultery, murder, breaking one of the ten commandments? Jesus said that the Holy Spirit convicts the world "of sin because they do not believe in Me." Not believing in Jesus is the unforgivable sin for which a person will be judged. Jesus told Nicodemus that God sent His Son into the world not to condemn the world, but that the world through Him might be saved. "He who believes in Him is not condemned; but he who does not believe is condemned already, because he has not believed in the name of the only begotten Son of God."[209] John the Baptist also bore testimony to that fact: "He who believes in the Son has everlasting life; and he who does not believe the Son shall not see life, but the wrath of God abides on him."[210] If a person refuses to believe that Jesus Christ is the Son of God who bore the sins of the whole world, they blaspheme the Holy Spirit by calling the Holy Spirit a liar. This is a profoundly serious matter. We read in Hebrews: "Of how much worse punishment, do you suppose, will he be thought worthy who has trampled the Son of God underfoot, counted the blood of the covenant by which he was sanctified a common thing, and insulted the Spirit of grace? For we know Him who said, *'Vengeance is Mine, I will repay,'* says the Lord. And again, *'The Lord* will judge His people.' It is a fearful thing to fall into the hands of the living God."[211] The Holy Spirit is in the world to convince you that Jesus Christ died on the cross for your sins, and that Jesus rose from the grave because His sacrifice in your place was sufficient. The whole sin issue is whether you believe in Jesus Christ – it makes the difference in being forgiven or being condemned.

The second task of the Holy Spirit in the world is to convict the world "of righteousness, because I go to My Father and you see Me no more." Now, sin is doing the wrong thing; righteousness is doing the right thing. Sin is missing the mark; righteousness is hitting the mark. Repeatedly, the Bible declares that the unrighteous will not get to heaven. It also declares that not one of us is righteous. So, what did Jesus mean? How did He equate righteousness with His ascension into heaven? When Jesus ascended into heaven, God bore public witness to the world that this was a man who lived a perfectly holy life, who always did the right thing, and that His righteousness granted Him entrance into heaven and that nothing short of this righteousness can grant anyone entrance into heaven. There is only one way any of us will gain entrance into heaven, and that is through the righteousness of Christ, imparted unto us by our faith and trust in Him alone.

Third, and finally, the Holy Spirit is convicting the world of judgment. But why did Jesus say, "of judgment, because the ruler of this world is judged?" The judgment Jesus described is not some future judgment, but a judgment that has already taken place. And where did that judgment take place? At the cross, as the apostle Paul confirmed to the believers at Colossae: "Having wiped out the handwriting of requirements that was against us, which was contrary to us. And He has taken it out of the way, having nailed it to the cross. Having disarmed principalities and powers, He made a public spectacle of them, triumphing over them in it."[212] Because Satan was judged at the cross, you are no longer subject to his dominion and control. You can be set free from bondage to sin because Jesus died to liberate you from the powers of darkness. Sin may be ended in your life when you place your faith and trust in His atoning death on the cross, His resurrection from among the dead, and His ascension to heaven, and allow the righteousness of Christ to be imparted to you. The power of the sinless life of Jesus makes it possible for you to live with God forever in heaven. And while here on earth, you do not have to live under the power and bondage of darkness any longer. Satan has been judged at the cross.

In addition to considering the work of the Holy Spirit in the world, let's also consider the current ministry of the Holy Spirit in the life of the believer. Jesus said of the Holy Spirit: "He will teach you all things and bring to your remembrance all things that I said to you."[213] In addition to being the private tutor for every believer, Jesus promised that the Holy Spirit would constantly remind us of what Jesus spoke to His disciples. On that same evening, Jesus told His disciples: "I still have many things to say to you, but you cannot bear *them* now. However, when He, the Spirit of truth, has come, He will guide you into all truth; for He will not speak on His own *authority*, but whatever He hears He will speak; and He will tell you things to come."[214] So, in addition to being our teacher and our reminder of the things that Jesus spoke, the Holy Spirit is guiding the believer into all truth and revealing the future to the believer. And our future is secure!

In his second letter to the believers living in Corinth, the apostle Paul alluded to the fact that God's deliverance is three-fold. He has delivered us from the penalty of sin; He is delivering us from the power of sin; and one day He will deliver us from the very presence of sin: "That we should not trust in ourselves but in God who raises the dead, who delivered us from so great a death, and does deliver us; in whom we trust that He will still deliver *us*."[215]

Paul brought the first phase of God's personal deliverance into focus in his letter to the believers who lived in Colossae: "He has delivered us from the power of darkness and conveyed *us* into the kingdom of the Son of His love, in whom we have redemption through His blood, the forgiveness of sins."[216] Paul also reminded the believers who lived in Galatia that He is currently delivering us from the power of sin: "Grace to you and peace from God the Father and our Lord Jesus Christ, who gave Himself for our sins, that He might deliver us from this present evil age, according to the will of our God and Father,"[217] And thirdly, Paul commended the believers living in Thessalonica for their patience while waiting for God's promise to deliver them one day from the very presence of evil: "How you turned to God from idols to serve the living and true God, and to wait for His Son from heaven, whom He raised from the dead, *even* Jesus who delivers us from the wrath to come."[218]

It is essential that we consider what Jesus had to say about how important knowing the truth would be to His followers and how to appropriate and develop the ability to discern fact from fiction. When confronted by His adversaries who tried to discredit Him publicly, He stated: "I am the light of the world. He who follows Me shall not walk in darkness but have the light of life."[219] Then He told those present who believed on Him: "If you abide in My word, you are My disciples indeed. And you shall know the truth, and the truth shall make you free. Therefore, if the Son makes you free, you shall be free indeed."[220] In other words, Jesus made a conditional promise regarding the truth. To appropriate the truth, we must follow Him who declared Himself to be: "The way, the truth, and the life,"[221] and saturate ourselves with the study of and obedience to His word and truly, genuinely become His disciple. The result will be the cultivation and development of our acuity of discernment which will prevent us from being entangled in lies and deception. We will be able to distinguish fact from fiction, reality from fantasy, truth from falsity, and honesty from dishonesty. We will not cave to chaos and confusion, nor compromise. We will not be stuck in the quicksand of popular opinion like Pontius Pilate was when he sarcastically responded to Jesus, "What is truth?"[222]

After raising her family as a stay-at-home mom, my mother trained and worked as a bank teller. Like most entry level bankers, part of her training included learning how to identify counterfeit currency. The method her employer used is still being used today. Tellers in training are assigned the task of counting stacks and stacks of paper bills, ones, fives, tens, twenties, fifties, and hundreds. The process allows the teller to become so familiar with genuine legal tender, that when the trainer slips in a counterfeit bill in a stack to be counted, the teller is trained to notice the difference, not by handling counterfeit currency, but by handling lots of genuine currency. The paradigm applies to the truth. The more we handle and become familiar with the truth and the source of the truth, the easier it is for us to recognize and identify the lies and falsities that get thrown at us.

Paul the apostle explained that the presence of the Holy Spirit in the church is also restraining Satan from unleashing his diabolical plans on the earth: "For the mystery of lawlessness is already at work; only He who now restrains *will do so* until He is taken out of the way."[223] The Holy Spirit is the One who is restraining the mystery of lawlessness. He is the One who is holding the lid on the boiling kettle of evil that, once released, will last for seven years.

WONDERS AND SIGNS

On the Day of Pentecost, as he quoted the prophecy of Joel, Peter declared: "'I will show wonders in heaven above and signs in the earth beneath: blood and fire and vapor of smoke. The sun shall be turned into darkness, and the moon into blood, before the coming of the great and awesome day of the Lord.'"[224] In other words, astronomical events and their occurrence will serve as God's three-dimensional billboard announcing the coming of the Prince of Peace and King of Kings.

On March 11th, 2015, our sun emitted an X-class solar flare and aimed a pillar of fire called a coronal mass ejection or CME directly at earth. NASA captured the image. Six days later, on March 17th, St. Patrick's Day, the charged particles emitted by the sun started colliding with earth causing mild to moderate radio interference and creating spectacular auroras visible in Scandinavia and as far south as Lake Michigan in the US and stunning when photographed by NASA astronauts aboard the International Space Station. Three days later - whether photographed in its totality by passengers aboard chartered jetliners high above the North Atlantic or its shadow cast upon the earth photographed by NASA astronauts aboard the International Space Station, what occurred on Friday, March 20, 2015, was the rarest of astronomical events. A total eclipse of the sun by a supermoon during the spring equinox. Let me try to explain. Because the orbit of our moon around earth is not circular, but elliptical, there are two distinct points in its orbit when it is the farthest from earth, called apogee, and the nearest to earth, called perigee. Thus, a supermoon occurs when the full moon is at perigee (its closest to the earth) and appears 16% bigger and 30% brighter than when the moon is at apogee (its farthest from the earth). A total solar eclipse by a supermoon is a rare astronomical occurrence. What was more extraordinary was the date of the eclipse. First, the date coincides with the spring (or vernal) equinox when the earth's axis is perpendicular to its orbital path around the sun and the sun's rays shine directly at the earth's equator. This allowed the total eclipse to be visible at the North Pole for just two minutes as the sun rose. The North Pole does not belong to any nation or people and is uninhabited, and as the path on a map shows, the total eclipse was visible mostly over open sea, and its path resembled the blade of a sickle. Second, the date of the solar eclipse coincided with Rosh Chodashim, the appearance of the new moon of spring which marks the first day of the Hebrew month Nisan - the beginning of the Hebrew religious calendar. That commemorates the date when the tabernacle in the wilderness was completed and dedicated to the Lord, and when heavenly fire came down and ignited the fire on the altar of sacrifice signifying God's presence within the tabernacle, which, as we have already seen, correlates with the pillars of fire that sat upon the heads of the disciples as they were all filled with the Holy Spirit on the Day of Pentecost.

Just two weeks after the total solar eclipse, when the new moon came between the sun and cast its shadow on the surface of the earth – the earth came between the sun and the moon and cast its shadow on the surface of the moon causing a total lunar eclipse. Have you ever seen a total lunar eclipse? The moon seems to turn red in the clear night sky, hence the name "blood moon." My wife,

Vickie, and I were leading a tour of the Holy Land and witnessed a total lunar eclipse in the night sky above Jerusalem on February 21, 2008. Considering what we read in the prophecy of Joel, the blood red moon seen over the City of Jerusalem was ominous. But what is even more ominous is the fact that in 2014 and 2015, there was a sequence of blood red moons that occurred on dates that are significant not only in the Hebrew calendar, but in the pattern of Jewish history and the fulfillment of Bible prophecy. The first total lunar eclipse and blood red moon occurred on the first day of Passover, April 15, 2014. The second was on the first day of Sukkot, October 8, 2014. Then on the date of the Hebrew new year, March 20, 2015, a total solar eclipse occurred. The third total lunar eclipse and blood red moon occurred on the first day of Passover, April 4, 2015. The fourth on the first day of Sukkot, September 28, 2015. These back-to-back astronomical events were the last of this century. Since Jesus Christ was born, eight back-to-back, blood-red moons have fallen on the first day of Passover and Sukkot. The fifth time was in 1493-94, when King Ferdinand and Queen Izabella expelled all the Jews from Spain, and dispatched Columbus, who discovered America; a safe haven for the Jews ever since. Terror to triumph. The sixth time was in 1949-50, right after the State of Israel was re-born and the Jews were victorious against the six Arab armies that attacked them. Terror to triumph. The seventh time was in 1967-68, when the Israelis were victorious once again in the six-day war and won the liberation of their eternal capital, Jerusalem. Terror to triumph.

What is even more extraordinary about the four blood moons in 2014-15 is that they also converged with a shemitah; the one year in seven when God commands the people of Israel to give the land rest. That sabbatical year began on the first day of the Jewish New Year, Rosh Hashanah, also the first day of the Feast of Trumpets, September 25, 2014, and ended on September 13, 2015, or Elul 29 in the Hebrew calendar. There is an interesting correlation between the shemitah, the sabbatical year, and the United States of America.

When speaking about prophecy, the most common question I get asked is "Where is America in Bible prophecy"? I am glad that I was born and reside in America – the land of the free and the home of the brave. But I must admit, America does not appear in the Bible narrative of the events of the last days. So, Denny, how could Bible prophecy be accurate if the only current superpower, the most prosperous and blessed country in the world, the greatest nation in human history, is left out of the Bible narrative of the events of the last days? Did God forget something? Doesn't He know how important a player on the world stage we are? The Bible tells us that nations are nothing to God; like the dust on a scale; so, as important as America might be to all of us, America is like the dust on a scale to God. The reality is that God has blessed America like no other nation in human history. From the indigenous people who were here long before the Europeans arrived; to the Christians who sought refuge from persecution as they settled here; to the founders who set these United States on a biblical foundation; to the pioneers who expanded the scope of this great land from sea to shining sea; to the men and women in uniform who gave the ultimate sacrifice to preserve the freedoms that we hold so dear; God has showered us with blessings throughout our history. Sadly, we have taken His blessings for granted and have forsaken the covenant our forefather's made with Him when they first arrived and signed the Mayflower Compact:

> Having undertaken, for the Glory of God, and advancements of the Christian faith and honor of our King and Country, a voyage to plant the first colony in the Northern parts of Virginia, do by these presents, solemnly and mutually, in the presence of God, and one another, covenant

and combine ourselves together into a civil body politic; for our better ordering, and preservation and furtherance of the ends aforesaid; and by virtue hereof to enact, constitute, and frame, such just and equal laws, ordinances, acts, constitutions, and offices, from time to time, as shall be thought most meet and convenient for the general good of the colony; unto which we promise all due submission and obedience.[225]

Their mission was officially dedicated to the glory of God by King James I of England:

We greatly commending, and graciously accepting of, their desires for the furtherance of so noble a work, which may, by the providence of Almighty God, hereafter tend to the glory of his divine Majesty, in propagating of Christian religion to such people, as yet live in darkness and miserable ignorance of the true knowledge and worship of God, and may in time bring the infidels and savages, living in those parts, to human civility, and to a settled and quiet government; Do, by these our letters pattents, graciously accept of, and agree to, their humble and well intended desires.[226]

ZEPHANIAH'S WARNING

That Tuesday dawned bright and clear in Ammon, Jordan. My wife and I were leading what was supposed to be the last day of a two-week tour of the Holy Land, and after visiting Petra the day before, we were excited about getting back to Israel and spending our final day in Jerusalem before heading to Ben-Gurien International Airport for our flight home. After a hearty breakfast at our hotel (As always, I loved the food and hospitality we enjoyed during our three days in Jordan), we boarded our bus and drove to the Allenby bridge crossing; said goodbye to our Jordanian tour guide and bus driver; and we were welcomed back to Israel by our Israeli tour guide, Miriam Feinberg Vamoosh and our Argentinian bus driver, Svika. After the long drive up from the Jordan River we arrived at the site of the Upper Room in Jerusalem, and to our surprise we joined a tour group from Applegate Christian Fellowship led by our good friend, Pastor Jon Courson. Pastor Jim Wright was playing his acoustic guitar and leading worship and our group joined in for a blessed time together. As we said farewell to one another and departed the Upper Room it was 4:30 in the afternoon.

Some people in our tour requested a visit to the bookstore at Gordon's Calvary, so Svika drove us to that location, and Vickie and I stayed on the bus as Miriam led our group to the bookstore and back. When Miriam got on the bus, she told us that the workers in the bookstore had been listening to BBC radio and informed our group that apparently, a small plane had crashed into one of the twin towers in New York City. While Miriam was telling us what she had heard, the two-way radio on our bus blared an urgent request in Hebrew for Miriam to call David Katz who served as the tour coordinator for Sar-El Travel at their office in Hebron. Vickie and I were sitting directly across from Miriam and watched her face turn ashen as she spoke with David. She looked at us and said in a hushed, stunned tone, "David says it is worse than any disaster movie you have ever seen." After she ended the call, she told us that an airliner had flown into the North Tower, and that a second airliner had flown into the South Tower. After securing Miriam's permission, Svika drove us to Tayelet Haas Promenade where we got off our bus and assembled on that spot with its spectacular view looking north to the old City of Jerusalem and together, we prayed for the peace of Jerusalem. When we arrived at our hotel just outside the Damascus gate, Jewish yeshiva students were watching the big screen television in the hotel lobby, and noticing our arrival, they immediately switched the channel to an English language station and together we watched in horror-filled silence the collapse of the North Tower at 10:28 am in New York City, 5:28 pm in Israel. Because the airways were completely shut down, our departure from Israel was delayed for five days. During those extra days, the hotel manager lodged us, fed us, and his hospitality staff laundered all our clothes (because we had been on the road for two weeks, we had no clean clothes). He explained that he was sorry that he could not let us stay for free, but he had to collect the hotel tax, which the government would charge him for our stay. His gracious and generous accommodation for our group will never be forgotten.

We watched and listened as the Jewish people wept with us and told us that now we would know what it is like to live under the constant threat of Islamic terrorism, all the while we heard the gunshots into the air and the trill of Muslim women celebrating as they passed out candy to passersby. Our hotel was just one block from the US Consulate, and we were there when PLO leader Yasser Arafat arrived to offer a donation of his blood for the survivors of the attacks on America. The contrast of the two reactions to that terrible day are forever indelibly imprinted in our memories. I spent many hours seeking the Lord for the significance of the events that had just unfolded on the world stage, and He led me in my research to several passages in the Bible that provided what I believe is a heavenly perspective.

When I was a boy growing up, my brothers and I would go down to the railroad tracks, put a penny on one of the tracks and then wait and listen. Long before we could see the train coming, we would hear the diesel locomotive approaching from the distance. It seemed like the whole earth shook as the engine finally arrived and its wheels flattened our pennies. He wasn't standing by a railroad track, but the ancient Hebrew prophet, Zephaniah, described the sights and sounds that would accompany the approach of the Day of the Lord.

Zephaniah served the Lord during the reign of King Josiah, and his message undoubtedly affected Josiah and prompted him to institute the reforms that were meaningful to the small remnant of true believers, even though the nation of Israel was destined for judgment. Zephaniah's message was unique. No other prophet painted a darker picture of God's judgment, and no prophet painted a brighter picture of Israel's future glory. Yet even within the warning concerning divine wrath, the prophet exhorted the people to seek the Lord, offering shelter amid judgment, and proclaiming the promise of eventual salvation for His believing remnant.

Have you ever stood on a mountain, looked out toward the horizon, and noticed the landscape – ridge after ridge separated by valleys between? Well, that is a good description of what Zephaniah saw as God spoke to him about the future. Zephaniah was given a message that would have its fulfillment in two phases – the first was the destruction of Jerusalem in 586 BC – but there was also a fulfillment in the distance that I believe is happening right now.

> The great day of the Lord is near; It is near and hastens quickly. The noise of the day of the Lord is bitter; there the mighty men shall cry out. That day *is* a day of wrath, a day of trouble and distress, a day of devastation and desolation, a day of darkness and gloominess, a day of clouds and thick darkness, a day of trumpet and alarm against the fortified cities and against the high towers. I will bring distress upon men, and they shall walk like blind men, because they have sinned against the Lord; Their blood shall be poured out like dust, and their flesh like refuse.

> Neither their silver nor their gold shall be able to deliver them.[227]

The prophetic images are identical to the events we all watched repeatedly that day – the cries of those who were brutally attacked – the wailing of the sirens as first responders rushed to the aid of those in danger - the immense dust clouds that filled the streets of New York City as the twin towers collapsed – the distress on the faces of those running away unable to see in the smoke and dust. I will never forget the story on the front page of the *New York Times* I saw once we landed and deplaned at Newark Liberty International Airport whose terminal lies directly across Newark Bay from ground zero. The article told the story of a truck driver who was hauling debris (loaded by hand in five-gallon buckets) from ground zero to the barges taking those buckets to the Fresh Kills Landfill for further inspection. On one of his many trips back and forth he unloaded a bucket that contained previously undiscovered body parts of a young child. The personal trauma his discovery had caused him made him quit his assignment. We wept as we read his story and we prayed for his recovery. While we read the article, we watched the smoke and dust still rising from ground zero and realized the validity of Zephaniah's ancient prophecy. I believe the tragic events of September 11, 2001, were just as Zephaniah had written 2,600 years ago; the noise of the train coming down the track, the bitter noise of destruction and desolation; but they were like smoke signals, too, letting us know that the Day of the Lord is rapidly approaching.

ISLAMIC TERRORISM

We all remember where we were and what we were doing, and how we were shaken by the videos shown repeatedly throughout that day. It did not take us long to discover the identities of those responsible; their images captured on security and surveillance cameras; and soon the FBI published the names and faces of the nineteen hijackers. They will be remembered in our world as evil men bent on carrying out their sinister plot even as they are revered as heroes in the Muslim world as *The Magnificent 19!* But who were these men? Where had they come from? Why did they sacrifice their own lives, and what had they hoped to accomplish? Truthfully, most Americans are ignorant about the answers to these questions. We have relied on Hollywood's portrayals of the Muslim world, movies like *Ali Baba and the Forty Thieves*, *Road to Morocco* starring Bob Hope, Dorothy Lamour, and Bing Crosby, or the Disney animated classic, *Aladdin* to provide us with information about the Muslim world. In our ignorance we have listened to and believed the lies that Islam is a peaceful religion, one of the great Monotheistic religions of the world. Author and film maker Gregory M. Davis who earned his Ph.D. in political science from Stanford University asserts:

> Contrary to the widespread insistence that true Islam is pacific even if a handful of its adherents are violent, Islamic sources make clear that engaging in violence against non-Muslims is a central and indispensable principle to Islam. Islam is less a personal faith than a political ideology that exists in a fundamental and permanent state of war with non-Islamic civilizations, cultures, and individuals. Those civilizations, cultures and individuals who do not submit to Islamic governance exist in an ipso facto state of rebellion with Allah and must be forcibly brought into submission. Islam achieves its full and proper form only when it assumes the powers of the state. It is important to distinguish that what we are talking about is not Islamic "fundamentalism,"

"fanaticism," nor "radical Islam," but Islam in its orthodox form as it has been understood and practiced by right-believing Muslims from the time of Mohammad to the present.[228]

Meanwhile, here at home, since 9/11, many more Americans have been killed in numerous separate acts of deadly Islamic terror or Islam-related honor killing in the United States. On November 5, 2009, US Army Major Nidal Malik Hasan, while serving as a psychiatrist at Fort Hood, Texas, opened fire on fellow service members and murdered thirteen and wounded twenty-nine. On April 15, 2013, two Islamic terrorist brothers, Dzhokhar, and Tamerlan Tsarnaev, placed homemade bombs near spectators at the finish line of the Boston Marathon and killed three and injured 180 people. On July 16, 2015, a lone jihadist gunned down five soldiers and wounded two others at a recruiting station in Chattanooga, Tennessee. The shooter, Muhammad Youssef Abdulazeez, was quoted saying, "Brothers and sisters don't be fooled by your desires, this life is short and bitter and the opportunity to submit to Allah may pass you by." On December 12, 2015, in San Bernardino, California, fourteen people were murdered and twenty-two seriously injured when Syed Rizwan Farook and Tashfeen Malik, a married couple with direct ties to ISIS, opened fire at an employee Christmas party. On June 13, 2016, fifty people were murdered, and fifty-three others were wounded at the Pulse Nightclub in Orlando, Florida as a lone gunman inspired by ISIS, committed the single most deadly mass shooting in U.S. history. On October 31, 2017, Sayfullo Saipov, who was inspired by ISIS, used a rented flatbed pickup truck to drive down a bike path in New York City and killed eight and injured eleven people. On December 6, 2019, Mohammed Saeed Alshamrani, an aviation student from Saudi Arabia, opened fire at the Naval Air Station in Pensacola, Florda. The attack, directed by al-Qaeda in the Arabian Peninsula, resulted in the death of three US Navy sailors and wounded eight. Additionally, hundreds of mass murder plots hatched by Islamic terrorists have been thwarted or botched.

I believe the Bible has something to say about what is going on. The Hebrew prophet, Jeremiah, heard a direct order from God: "For thus says the Lord God of Israel to me: 'Take this wine cup of fury from My hand, and cause all the nations, to whom I send you, to drink it. And they will drink and stagger and go mad because of the sword that I will send among them.'"[229] Did you know that there are over two hundred words used for *sword* in the Arabic language? Could Islamic terrorism be the sword that God told the prophet Jeremiah that He would send against all nations? Let's consider the recent history of Islamic imperialism and its relationship with the United States.

A sometime teacher and watch repairman in Egypt, Hasan al-Banna, founded the Society of the Muslim Brothers, more commonly called the Muslim Brotherhood in 1928. Their logo displays crossed swords beneath a depiction of the Quran. By the late 1940s, the Muslim Brotherhood had established some 2,000 branches throughout Egypt boasting about one million members and sympathizers, where their motto resonated: "Allah is our goal; the Quran is our constitution, the Prophet is our leader; Jihad is our way; and death in the path of Allah is our highest aspiration." The Muslim Brotherhood's stated objectives were individual moral purification and collective political and social regeneration through the establishment of a truly Islamic government in Egypt, as a springboard for universal expansion "until the entire world will chant the name of the Prophet [Muhammad], Allah's prayers and blessings be upon him."

One of those early alliances was with Amin al-Husseini, the Grand Mufti of Jerusalem, and Yassar Arafat's uncle. In 1933, al-Husseini contacted the Nazi's about supplying recruits for the Waffen-SS, the military wing of the Nazi party. Not only did the alliance between al-Husseini and Hassan al-Banna provide plenty of Muslim recruits, but it also endeared the Muslim Brotherhood to the Nazi party and to the Nazi leader himself, Adolf Hitler. History records for us that Hitler was partly motivated to invade the Soviet Union to capture the oil-rich Caucasus region inhabited by Muslim minorities. When the German army seized the North Caucasus in 1942, their slaughter of Jewish residents and their re-opening of the mosques that had been closed by the Soviets was cheered by the Muslims who lived there. Meanwhile, hundreds of thousands of Muslim soldiers who had been conscripted into the Soviet army were captured by the advancing German army and became prisoners of war. At first, they were treated poorly by their German captors. A German officer and Uzbek ex-pat living in Germany, Veli Kayum, entered the camps and enlisted their aid in forming fighting military units to combat their former Soviet masters. As the war raged on, Muslim men saw the opportunity to fight alongside of the German army against Stalin as a chance to re-pay the Soviets for the persecution many of them had faced. And so, many Muslim men enlisted in the German army where they were allowed to practice their Islamic faith and allied themselves with Nazi efforts to exterminate Jews. And thus, al-Husseini, al-Banna, and Heinrich Himmler together celebrated the concept of "The Final Solution," the extermination of all Jews everywhere.

With the surrender of the Nazi's and the end of WWII in Europe, it was now turn for America to exploit the anti-Soviet sentiments of the Muslim population in the Soviet Union. Little did we know what would develop as we pursued that strategy. At first, the US concentrated on working with ex-Nazi, non-Russian Muslim emigres as part of a CIA-funded broadcast organization, Radio Liberty, headquartered in Germany and dedicated to the overthrow of the Soviet Union. Radio Free Europe was an enterprise that the former leader of the Allied victory in Europe, President Eisenhower, supported fully. His administration's main concern was the growing nuclear threat that the Soviet Union posed to the free world.

In September 1953, during Eisenhower's first term, the Library of Congress and Princeton University jointly sponsored "a meeting between leading Islamic intellectuals and Americans interested in the Moslem world." Prior to the conference, Muslim leaders requested a meeting with President Eisenhower who was keen to influence the Muslim world. The overt goal of the conference was to promote an Islamic "Renaissance," but it also served to cement US relations with the Muslim Brotherhood.

The leader of the Muslim Brotherhood at that time was Dr. Said Ramadan. To facilitate his inclusion in the visit to the White House and the conference, the US Embassy in Cairo sanitized Ramadan's career history to eliminate his close association with the Grand Mufti, al-Husseini, and hide the fact that he was the son-in-law of Hassan al-Banna, the founder of the Muslim Brotherhood. Despite viewing the West as degenerate, Said Ramadan and the Grand Mufti viewed Soviet Communism as the foremost enemy of Islam. In the views of the US, that made Ramadan an influential Muslim anti-communist.

Deputy Director of the US Information Agency, Abbott Washburn, recalled the high priority that Eisenhower gave to religion in his personal life and in geopolitical strategy. He sent a note to Eisenhower's psychological warfare whiz, C.D. Jackson: "That the Princeton Islamic Colloquium might achieve a hoped for result that the Muslims will be impressed with the moral and spiritual strength of America. These individuals can exert a profound and far-reaching impact upon Muslim thinking. Their long-term influence may well outweigh that of the political leaders of their countries."

After the meeting at Princeton, the CIA subsequently did an analysis of Ramadan at the conference and concluded that "Ramadan seems to be a fascist, interested in power. He did not display many ideas except for those of the Muslim

Brotherhood." Despite that skepticism, because of the Eisenhower administration's concern with the growing Soviet influence in Egypt under Gamal Nassar, our government supported the Muslim Brotherhood during Eisenhower's second term. In a letter to Presbyterian Church leader Edward Elson, Eisenhower wrote: "I assure you that I never fail in any communication with Arab leaders, oral or written, to stress the importance of the spiritual factor in our relationships. I have argued that belief in God should create between them and us the common purpose of opposing atheistic communism."[230]

The real motivating factor was the possibility of jihad against Communism. Eisenhower spoke about this in a memo written by his staff summarizing discussions with the CIA covert ops chief, Frank Wisner. The memo notes: "The President said ... we should do everything possible to stress the 'holy war' aspect. Mr. Dulles commented that if Arabs have a 'holy war' they would want it to be against Israel. The President recalled, however, that [King Ibn] Saud ... had called on all Arabs to oppose Communism."[231] The result of this dialog in the highest office of the USA was a continuation of the pursuit to recruit Muslims by our government to the cause of fighting communism. With an attempted 1954 assassination plot by the Muslim Brotherhood on the life of Egyptian strongman Gamal Abdel Nasser, Ramadan fled Egypt for Saudi Arabia.

Pulitzer-prize winning author, Ian Johnson, describes in his book, *A Mosque in Munich*, how on the day after Christmas in 1958, Ramadan met with the ex-Nazi Muslim soldiers and several Muslim students seeking to establish an Islamic Center in Munich, Germany. He then began proselytizing widely about fighting communism to raise money for construction of the mosque. He secured funding for the building from Saudi Arabia, Libya, Jordan, and Turkey. The United States had wanted a credible voice in the Muslim world to fight communism and they found it with Ramadan. As he developed strong anti-Communist credentials, Ramadan was able to increase the influence of the Muslim Brotherhood and internationalize the German Muslims and the mosque in Munich.

From that European center, the Muslim Brotherhood spawned many organizations in America. In 1962, they formed the oldest Muslim Brotherhood front in the US, the Muslim Student Association. The first MSA National chapter was formed in 1963 at the campus of University of Illinois at Urbana-Champaign, which launched the Islamic Society of North America. The National MSA has grown to more than several hundred chapters on high school, college and university campuses throughout the US and Canada. The establishment of those bases of operation spawned the current pro-Palestinian protests and the reprehensible vocal public support for Hamas and the eruption of antisemitism on college and university campuses across America. All those efforts also set up the mosque in Munich for the next stage. In 1973, alleged al-Qaeda financier Youssef Nada took over management of the Munich Mosque and led it into the Saudi network. In 1977, they created the International Institute of Islamic Thought (IIIT) to nurture and spread the neo-Salafist doctrine of Hassan al-Bana and others.

In 1979, unthwarted by our previous miscalculations, once again we found ourselves supporting Muslims against the Soviets. This time, in Afghanistan. That effort was spawned by National Security Adviser Zbigniew Brzezinski under President Carter and was another anti-Soviet attempt to use a "holy war," along with billions from the US, the Saudis, and the corrupt Pakistani Inter-Service Intelligence service, to weaken the USSR. After the Soviet 40th Army retreated from Afghanistan in 1989, al Qaeda, followers of the Muslim Brotherhood Islamic doctrine, arose to afflict us with global Islamic terror. Their first target on American soil was New York City, and on February 26, 1993, a truck bomb was detonated below the North Tower of the World Trade Center which killed six people and injured thousands. On August 7, 1998, two simultaneous explosions destroyed the American embassies in Nairobi, Kenya, and Dar es Saalem, Tanzania, killing 224 people and injuring over 4,500. On October 12, 2000, seventeen U.S. Navy sailors were killed when the U.S. Navy destroyer, USS Cole, was bombed by Islamic terrorists while refueling in the port of Aden in Yemen.

Implicated in the 9/11 attacks, Youssef Nada's villa in Lugano, Switzerland, was searched for evidence in November 2001. The government found key documents now called, "The Project," a twelve-point plan, dated December 1, 1982, to launch a "cultural invasion" and eventual conquest of the West to establish a worldwide Islamic state under Sharia.

Jerry Gordon, a former U.S. Army Intelligence officer and Sr. Editor at *New English Review* concluded: "What we have learned in this cautionary tale of early US involvement with the Muslim Brotherhood during the Cold War era, is how nearsighted this country's leaders have been about the international political agenda of the Ikhwan. Hopes to use the Muslim Brotherhood in a 'holy war' against Soviet Communism backfired."[232] First in our support for Said Ramadan, and the feckless nature of the CIA during the secret war in Afghanistan with Saudi partners against Soviet forces. But has the Muslim Brotherhood's influence in America grown stronger or weaker? According to author, Erick Stakelbeck, in his book *The Brotherhood – America's Next Great Enemy*, the Muslim Brotherhood should be regarded as an existential threat.

In 2009, President Obama was in Cairo where he delivered a speech titled *A New Beginning* to a receptive audience at the Major Reception Hall at Cairo University in Egypt. The President infuriated Egyptian President Hosni Mubarak by inviting leaders of the Muslim Brotherhood. Egypt was chosen for Obama's speech because as then White House Press Secretary Robert Gibbs said, "it is a country that in many ways represents the heart of the Arab world." But, as you now know, Egypt was the birthplace of the

Muslim Brotherhood. Soon after President Obama's speech in Cairo, demonstrations and riots erupted in Tahrir Square in Cairo which led to the return from thirty years of exile of the Muslim Brotherhood's spiritual leader, Sheikh Yusuf Qaradawi, who addressed a crowd in Tahrir Square estimated at two million where he raised the banner of jihad. Before President Obama's speech in Cairo, Qaradawi wrote an open letter to the President arguing Islamic terrorism is a direct response to U.S. foreign policy. Soon after the return of Qaradawi, Egyptian President, Hosni Mubarak was overthrown and arrested and the Muslim Brotherhood's candidate, Mohamed Morsi, was elected President.

In August of 2004, an alert Maryland Transportation Authority Police officer observed a woman wearing traditional Islamic garb videotaping the support structures of the Chesapeake Bay Bridge and conducted a traffic stop. The driver was Ismail Elbarasse and he was detained on an outstanding material witness warrant issued in Chicago in connection with fundraising for Hamas. The FBI's Washington Field Office subsequently executed a search warrant on Elbarasse's residence in Annandale, Virginia. In the basement of his home, a hidden sub-basement was found; it revealed over eighty banker boxes of the archives of the Muslim Brotherhood in North America.

One of the most important of these documents made public to date was entered into evidence during the Holy Land Foundation trial. It amounted to the Muslim Brotherhood's strategic plan for the United States and was entitled, *An Explanatory Memorandum: On the General Strategic Goal for the Group in North America*. The Explanatory Memorandum was written in 1991 by a member of the Board of Directors for the Muslim Brotherhood in North America and senior Hamas leader named Mohammed Akram. It had been approved by the Brotherhood's Shura Council and Organizational Conference and was meant for internal review by the Brotherhood's leadership in Egypt. It was certainly not intended for public consumption, particularly in the targeted society: the

United States. For these reasons, the memo constitutes a Rosetta stone for the Muslim Brotherhood, its goals, modus operandi, and infrastructure in America. It is arguably the single most important vehicle for understanding a secretive organization and should, therefore, be considered required reading for policymakers and the public, alike.

The memorandum exposed the strategy being employed in the USA by the Muslim Brotherhood:

> The process of settlement is a 'Civilization-Jihadist Process' with all the word means. The Ikhwan must understand that their work in America is a kind of grand jihad in eliminating and destroying the Western civilization from within and 'sabotaging' its miserable house by their hands and the hands of the believers so that it is eliminated, and God's religion is made victorious over all other religions. The success of the Movement in America in establishing an observant Islamic base with power and effectiveness will be the best support and aid to the global Movement project.[233]

The goal is to get rid of the non-Islamic political order and replace it with the order of Islamic law.

In the words of Albrecht Hauser: "If the West puts its collective head in the sand by denying the danger that political and militant Islam represents for liberally conceived civil society, its own refusal to act with seriousness will lead to bondage and dehumanization."[234]

Amid our national ignorance and lack of vigilance regarding these threats, I just want you to know that I believe I can hear the train that is comin'!

ZEPHANIAH'S WARNINGS - PART 2

After the terrorist attack on 9/11, President Bush declared a National Day of Prayer and Presidents past and present and their families gathered at our National Cathedral in Washington, DC. Spiritual leaders gathered to intercede before they led us in national repentance and prayer just as the Lord had warned His people in Zephaniah's day. But, if we fail to understand the significance of these events in the light of scripture, we do so at our own peril. Zephaniah warned the citizens of Israel before judgment fell upon them: "Gather yourselves together, yes, gather together, O undesirable nation, before the decree is issued, *or* the day passes like chaff, before the Lord's fierce anger comes upon you, before the day of the Lord's anger comes upon you! Seek the Lord, all you meek of the earth, who have upheld His justice. Seek righteousness, seek humility. It may be that you will be hidden in the day of the Lord's anger."[235]

God went on to reveal to Zephaniah something that I believe is happening right now. "For Gaza shall be forsaken, and Ashkelon desolate; they shall drive out Ashdod at noonday, and Ekron shall be uprooted. I have heard the reproach of Moab, and the insults of the people of Ammon, with which they have reproached My people, and made arrogant threats against their borders."[236] Part of Zephaniah's prophecy was fulfilled via an intriguing story of betrayal. In 2002, the Quartet (USA, EU, Russia, and UN) had put together a new plan to revive the Middle East peace process and called it *The Road Map*. It called for the creation of two states and for the Palestinians to stop using terrorism. Under intense pressure from President Bush and Secretary of State Condoleezza Rice, Israeli Prime Minister Ariel Sharon proved that Israel was willing to make very painful concessions to achieve peace, and he ordered the mandatory evacuation of Gaza in August 2005, uprooting in the process more than 8,000 Israelis who had called it home since 1967. Jewish families who had lived, worked, and played alongside Muslim families for generations were forced to evacuate their homes, their schools, their businesses, all for the prospects of peace with the Palestinians. It is no laughing matter, this whole issue of land for peace. Just ask any Native American.

Iran exploited the Israeli forced evacuation from Gaza and planned, supported, and trained Hamas, the radical Islamist terrorist organization, to take over the role of ruler in Gaza from the PLO. Initially, Hamas used Iranian funds to help the Palestinian residents with benefits that won Hamas a majority in free elections, and then used force to keep those residents in bondage to the publicly declared objective of destroying Israel and annihilating the Jews. In horrific testimony to their charter, on October 7, 2023, Hamas terrorists launched a brutal attack on Israel, simultaneously launching thousands of their unguided rockets and by air, land, and sea invading the Israeli communities near Gaza and committing acts of barbarism against soldiers, police, and innocent civilians. In response to the unspeakable atrocities Hamas committed, Israel has vowed to eliminate all Hamas personnel in Gaza and retake the land they were pressured by the US Government to vacate in 2005.

I believe that the Lord has sent us warnings about coming judgment. On September 11, 2001, the entire world watched as the towers of the World Trade Center in New York City eventually collapsed and the dust and smoke rose over the harbor and the watchful gaze of the Statue of Liberty. And for three weeks, churches in America were packed. But we were told to go back to life as normal – and verses from the Bible were quoted by our political leaders telling us that "we will rebuild." For those of you who have read Rabbi Jonathan Cahn's books, *The Harbinger*, and *The Mystery of the Shemitah*, or watched the movie he released, *The Isaiah 9:10 Judgment*, or for those of you who have read Pastor Mark Biltz's book, *Blood Moons*, you are familiar with what I am telling you. Both authors make a correlation between the shemitah, the sabbatical year and events in America's history.

According to *Time* magazine, following the worst terrorist attack in U.S. history on Sept. 11, the US Stock market plummeted 684 points, or 7%, on its first day of trading. The date? The answer depends on what calendar you use - 9/17/01 in the Gregorian calendar, or Elul 29 in the Hebrew calendar. Seven years later, the U.S. House of Representatives' failure to pass the Bush Administration's $700 billion bailout plan triggered the biggest one-day point drop in the history of the Dow Jones industrial average. The market plummeted 777 points, or 7%. The date? The answer depends on what calendar you use -9/29/08 in the Gregorian calendar, or Elul 29 in the Hebrew calendar.

THREE PHASES

In the light of coming deliverance, what is important for us to consider is the fact that on the Day of Pentecost, Peter stopped quoting Joel's prophecy before Joel's prophecy was finished. Let's compare what Peter said on the Day of Pentecost with what God revealed to the prophet Joel hundreds of years earlier. Peter began by quoting a portion of Joel chapter 2:

> And it shall come to pass afterward that I will pour out My Spirit on all flesh; your sons and your daughters shall prophesy, your old men shall dream dreams, your young men shall see visions. And also on *My* menservants and on *My* maidservants I will pour out My Spirit in those days. And I will show wonders in the heavens and in the earth: blood and fire and pillars of smoke. The sun shall be turned into darkness, and the moon into blood, before the coming of the great and awesome day of the Lord. And it shall come to pass *that* whoever calls on the name of the Lord shall be saved.[237]

Now, please notice that this is where Peter stopped when he quoted this prophecy on the Day of Pentecost – but God was not finished speaking to Joel. Let's read the beginning of the rest of what the Lord said to Joel – the second part of verse 32: "For in Mount Zion and in Jerusalem there shall be deliverance, as the Lord has said, among the remnant whom the Lord calls."[238] The rest of the prophecy beginning here and continuing through chapter 3 pertains to the deliverance of Israel through the Tribulation and into the 1,000-year reign of Christ on earth from Jerusalem. So, why did Peter stop quoting the prophecy in midstream? I believe the Holy Spirit prompted Peter to stop because the Lord wanted to reveal that there are two distinct phases to His plan of deliverance.

I have often said that the best commentary on the Bible is the Bible. Several years after Peter had spoken the words of part of Joel's prophecy the church was confronted with a dilemma – Gentiles were coming to faith in Jesus Christ by droves, and many in the church who were formerly Jews were concerned, so a meeting was held in Jerusalem: "And after they had become silent, James answered, saying, 'Men and brethren, listen to me: Simon has declared how God at the first visited the Gentiles to take out of them a people for His name. And with this the words of the prophets agree, just as it is written: 'After this I will return and will rebuild the tabernacle of David, which has fallen down; I will rebuild its ruins, and I will set it up; so that the rest of mankind may seek the Lord, even all the Gentiles who are called by My name, says the Lord who does all these things.'"[239] James explained the 3 phases of God's plan of deliverance.

FIRST - THE CHURCH

The first phase is what is happening right now – God is taking out of the nations a people for His name – Jesus is busy building

His church. And once that work is finished, God will remove the church from the earth and once again deal directly with the nation of Israel and deliver them through the Tribulation.

SECOND - ISRAEL

The Lord revealed the second phase of God's plan of deliverance and the foremost purpose of the Tribulation to Jeremiah the prophet: "Alas! For that day *is* great, so that none *is* like it; and it *is* the time of Jacob's trouble, but he shall be saved out of it."[240] God's purpose for Israel in the Tribulation is to bring about the conversion of a multitude of Jews, who will enter the blessings of the kingdom and experience personally the fulfillment of all the covenants that pertain to Israel. The good news that the King is about to return will be preached so that all the nations of the earth may be turned to their deliverer. Just as John the Baptist preached just such a message to prepare Israel for the first coming of the Messiah, as God revealed to Malachi: "Behold, I will send you Elijah the prophet before the coming of the great and dreadful day of the Lord. And he will turn the hearts of the fathers to the children, and the hearts of the children to their fathers, lest I come and strike the earth with a curse."[241]

THIRD - THE GENTILES

The third phase of God's plan of deliverance is God's purpose to populate the millennium with a multitude of saved Gentiles, who are redeemed by the preaching of the believing remnant, just as James said when he quoted the prophecy given to Amos: "*so that the rest of mankind may seek the Lord,* even all the Gentiles who are called by My name, says the Lord who does all these things.'"[242]

THE THIRD TEMPLE

And the prophecy given to Amos was specific: "On that day I will raise up the tabernacle of David, which has fallen down, and repair its damages; I will raise up its ruins and rebuild it as in the days of old;"[243] The Lord revealed that the restoration of the Hebrew Temple in Jerusalem was key to God's plan to deliver Israel.

EZEKIEL'S PROPHECIES

God also revealed the steps along the way to the prophet Ezekiel: Allow me to provide an outline of the prophecies God gave to Ezekiel in chapters 36-40: chapter 36 – the renewal of the ancient land of Israel and the return of the children of Israel to the land. Chapter 37 – the resurrection of the people of Israel and the reunification of the tribes of Israel. Chapters 38-39 – the rescue of the people of Israel and Chapter 40 - the rebuilding of the Temple of God in Israel.

This book does not permit us to dive into the details of God's prophecy in Ezekiel chapters 38-39, so please let me outline these chapters and then bring us full circle as it has to do with the Lord's plan to deliver Israel:

A Russian-led Islamic confederation invades Israel.

God ravages Russia and the USA.

God miraculously rescues Israel.

The Russian-led Islamic alliance is made of ancient Persia – modern-day Iran, ancient Ethiopia – modern-day Sudan, Libya, ancient Gomer – the Turkic nations, and ancient Togarmah – modern-day Turkey. Some commentators that I respect believe that Ezekiel 38-39, the invasion of Israel by Gog, is part of the war of Armageddon – but the clear teaching of the Bible refutes that conclusion: The Russian-led invasion comes from the north – the final battle of Armageddon comes from every point on the compass. As we read in Ezekiel 38:15: "Then you will come from your place out of the far north, you and many peoples with you," However, in Armageddon – "go out to the kings of the earth and of the whole world, to gather them to the battle of that great day of God Almighty" – Rev. 16:14.

The Russian-led invasion is a limited alliance that comes to "take plunder" – the war of Armageddon is a clash of all the armies in the world against Christ. Just as we read in Ezekiel 38:12 – "to take plunder and to take booty," versus what we read about the battle of Armageddon in Rev. 19:19: "their armies, gathered together to make war against Him who sat on the horse and against His army."

The conclusion of the Russian-led invasion is vastly different from the conclusion of the war of Armageddon. First, the way the invading force is defeated is different. In Ezekiel 38:22 we read: The invading force is defeated by "pestilence and bloodshed," whereas in Armageddon, the invading force is defeated by the Lord Jesus Christ Himself, Rev. 19:20-21. Second, the way the invading force is devoured is different. In Ezekiel 39:17 we read: Birds and beasts devour the invading force, whereas in Armageddon, the invading force is devoured by birds only, Rev. 19:17-18.

The results of the Russian-led invasion are vastly different from the result of the war of Armageddon. First, God's response to the attack will be different. In Ezekiel 39:6 we read: "And I will send fire on Magog and on those who live in security in the coastlands." whereas in Armageddon, Isaiah 66:18-24 declares Christ will summon those who dwell in the coastlands. Second, Satan's role in each is different. In the Ezekiel conflict, we learn from reading 2 Thessalonians 2:1-10 and Rev. 12:1-12 that Satan's man is revealed and Satan himself is released on the earth for 1,260 days. Whereas, as a result of Armageddon, Satan is bound for 1,000 years - Rev. 20:1-3. Third, and finally, the Temple's role is different in each: In the Ezekiel conflict, Ezekiel

40-48 & Daniel 9:26-27 describe the rebuilding of the Temple and "the abomination that makes desolate" Whereas because of Armageddon, Rev. 20:4-6 describe the restoration and occupation of the Temple by the King of Kings.

It is unmistakable – the world is heading toward a world war that will bring global devastation and set the stage for the Tribulation – that seven-year period Jeremiah called, "The time of Jacob's trouble." But remember, God will deliver Israel through it. "The Gentiles shall know that the house of Israel went into captivity for their iniquity; because they were unfaithful to Me, therefore I hid My face from them. I gave them into the hands of their enemies, and they all fell by the sword. According to their uncleanness and according to their transgressions I have dealt with them and hidden My face from them."[244]

But the Lord also told Ezekiel that His miraculous defeat of the invading force from the north will usher in Israel's restoration: "And I will not hide My face from them anymore; for I shall have poured out My Spirit on the house of Israel,' says the Lord God."[245] That will fulfill God's promise of the latter rain as prophesied: "Be glad then, you children of Zion, And rejoice in the LORD your God; For He has given you the former rain faithfully, And He will cause the rain to come down for you—The former rain, And the latter rain in the first *month.*"[246] Remember, the former rain was fulfilled when the Holy Spirit was poured out upon those 120 Jewish disciples in the Upper Room in Jerusalem on the Day of Pentecost. The latter rain will be fulfilled when God pours out His Holy Spirit upon the 144,000 of Revelation 7:1-8.

Paul the apostle wrote about that wonderful day: "For I do not desire, brethren, that you should be ignorant of this mystery, lest you should be wise in your own opinion, that blindness in part has happened to Israel until the fullness of the Gentiles has come in. And so all Israel will be saved, as it is written: *'The Deliverer will come out of Zion, and He will turn away ungodliness from Jacob; for this is My covenant with them, when I take away their sins.'*"[247]

No wonder the Lord told Moses how the priests were to bless the children of Israel: "And the Lord spoke to Moses, saying: 'Speak to Aaron and his sons, saying, 'This is the way you shall bless the children of Israel. Say to them: 'The Lord bless you and keep you; the Lord make His face shine upon you and be gracious to you; the Lord lift up His countenance upon you, and give you peace.' So, they shall put My name on the children of Israel, and I will bless them."[248]

THE USA

Let's turn our attention homeward, and considered the question I get asked more than any other when it comes to Bible prophecy – "Where is America in Bible prophecy?" As Hal Lindsay wrote in the 1970's in his benchmark boob, *The Late Great Planet Earth*; as Dr. Chuck Missler has written more recently in his book, *Prophecy 2020*; and as Dr. Mark Hitchcock, who studied under John Valvoord, has written in his book, *The Late Great United States*; although a list of nations and confederations are named specifically in scripture's revelation of the future, America is not. Thus, we may conclude that something dramatic must happen to America.

There are those that believe America is going down the drain, caught in a vortex that is irreversible even while others believe that there is a new day dawning in America that will see her rise and be great again. So, Denny, which view do you take? Great question. I am not sure. But I do believe that America's future is in our hands right now, just like the fate of the nation of Israel was decided by what the people did in response to what the Lord told them through His prophet, Jeremiah over 2,500 years ago:

> The word which came to Jeremiah from the Lord,
> saying: "Arise and go down to the potter's house,

and there I will cause you to hear My words." Then I went down to the potter's house, and there he was, making something at the wheel. And the vessel that he made of clay was marred in the hand of the potter; so he made it again into another vessel, as it seemed good to the potter to make. Then the word of the Lord came to me, saying: "O house of Israel, can I not do with you as this potter?" says the Lord. "Look, as the clay *is* in the potter's hand, so *are* you in My hand, O house of Israel! The instant I speak concerning a nation and concerning a kingdom, to pluck up, to pull down, and to destroy *it*, if that nation against whom I have spoken turns from its evil, I will relent of the disaster that I thought to bring upon it. And the instant I speak concerning a nation and concerning a kingdom, to build and to plant it, if it does evil in My sight so that it does not obey My voice, then I will relent concerning the good with which I said I would benefit it. Now therefore, speak to the men of Judah and to the inhabitants of Jerusalem, saying, 'Thus says the Lord: 'Behold, I am fashioning a disaster and devising a plan against you. Return now every one from his evil way, and make your ways and your doings good.' And they said, 'That is hopeless! So we will walk according to our own plans, and we will every one obey the dictates of his evil heart.'[249]

Jeremiah 18 is the sad account of how God dealt with the nation of Israel when they forgot and forsook God and refused to heed His warnings about impending judgment. History records the consequence: Israel was taken away as a nation and exiled to Babylon. In my opinion, these words spoken by God to His prophet, Jeremiah, speak volumes about where America is at presently. God is gracious and merciful and has demonstrated His lovingkindness in immeasurable ways to this nation of ours. But just as the first vessel, we have become marred in the potter's hands. Thus, God is not obligated in any way to provide the benefits His Word has promised that nation whose God is the Lord. In fact, I believe the time is late, and God has provided one final warning: "Behold, I am fashioning a disaster and devising a plan against you. Return now every one of you from his evil way, and make your ways and your doings good." Sadly, our response sounds like the children of Israel's, "That is hopeless! So we will walk according to our own plans, and we will every one obey the dictates of his evil heart." That is indeed a scary thought, isn't it? You see, this passage in Jeremiah reminds us that God is absolutely sovereign – sovereign among individuals, and sovereign among nations, just as the Lord revealed to His prophet, Isaiah: "Behold, the nations *are* as a drop in a bucket, and are counted as the small dust on the scales; All nations before Him *are* as nothing, and they are counted by Him less than nothing and worthless"[250] Americans have an exaggerated sense of our own importance in the world. Our nation's power, prosperity, and peace are the direct result of God's blessings – but remember the clay on the potter's wheel. If the clay on the potter's wheel is marred for one use, it shall serve for another; those nations that will not be made monuments of His mercy shall be made monuments of His judgment!

In his benchmark book, *When a Nation Forgets God – 7 Lessons We Must Learn from Nazi Germany,* Dr. Erwin D. Lutzer, Senior Pastor of Moody Bible Church in Chicago, Illinois, parallels the changes taking place in America today with the changes that transformed Germany less than one hundred years ago. In the book, he relates how the church was compromised; how Hitler, a baptized Catholic, mocked the Protestant pastors, "You can do anything you want with them. They will submit. They are insignificant little people, submissive as dogs, and they sweat with embarrassment when you talk to them." Lutzer wrote about how the economic collapse in Germany after WWI spurred by hyper-inflation brought about by the German government's printing of money facilitated the government's takeover of the economy including a nationalized healthcare system and how individual freedoms were surrendered to the state in exchange for the necessities of life. How the laws were changed to remove God from government – even forbidding the word *Christmas* and changing the date from December 25th to December 21st to celebrate paganism; and how the silence of the saints provided Hitler little resistance to his evil agenda.

So, what is America's future? The more important question we should ask, "What is your future here in America?" The Christian church has suffered throughout its' existence, so would we be terribly surprised if now it is our turn? Like the early Christians, I believe that someday, sooner than we imagine, we will find that our commitment to share the good news of Jesus Christ will run counter to the laws of the land. We had better be prepared to answer these questions: At what point do we have to become breakers of our laws rather than betrayers of our Lord? At what price are we willing to take the Cross into the world and identify with our Savior? How do we love the people of the world and yet oppose the agenda of those who would silence the gospel?

First, we must acknowledge that our public effectiveness is a by-product of our private and personal relationship with God. As renowned author and lecturer Os Guinness said: "There is no problem in the wider culture that you cannot see in spades in the church. The rot is in us, and not simply out there. It's a much deeper crisis." He also said: "America is in danger of squandering what is at the heart of its great heritage. Religious liberty is endangered by those who reduce freedom of conscience and the free exercise of religion to freedom of worship, who seek to remove religion from the public square, and who rebrand disagreement as discrimination and religious conviction as bigotry."[251]

I have stood beneath the monolithic statue of Dr. King at his memorial in Washington, DC and have read his words engraved on the north wall: "The ultimate measure of a man is not where he stands in moments of convenience and comfort, but where he stands at times of challenge and controversy." We have read his words engraved on the south wall: "Darkness cannot drive out darkness, only light can do that. Hate cannot drive out hate, only love can do that." Both are quotes from a speech he gave in 1963, the year I became a teenager. It has been sixty years since Dr. King's assassination – killed as he was standing on the second-floor balcony of the Lorraine Hotel in Memphis, Tennessee by a single bullet from a rifle fired from a bathroom window in a boarding house room by James Earl Ray. Just five years before his assassination, on April 12, 1963, Martin Luther King Jr was arrested following a nonviolent protest demonstrating against segregation in Birmingham Alabama. Police Commissioner Eugene "Bull" Connor arrested King for demonstrating without a permit and placed him in the Birmingham City Jail for six days. On the day of his arrest, a group of clergymen wrote an open letter in which they called for the community to renounce protest tactics that caused unrest in the community, to do so in court and "not in the streets." It was that letter that prompted King to draft, on April 16, the famous document known as *Letter from a Birmingham Jail*. In that long letter, Dr. King wrote:

> There was a time when the church was very powerful – in the time when the early Christians rejoiced at deemed being worthy to suffer for what they believed. In those days, the church was not merely a thermometer that recorded the ideals and principles of popular opinion; it was a thermostat that transformed the mores of society. Whenever

the early Christians entered a town, the people in power became disturbed and immediately sought to convict the Christians for being 'disturbers of the peace' and 'outside agitators.' But the Christians pressed on, in the conviction that they were a 'colony from heaven,' called to obey God rather than man. Small in number, they were big in commitment. They were too God-intoxicated to be 'astronomically intimidated.' By their effort and example they brought an end to such ancient evils as infanticide and gladiatorial contests.

Those who would choose to remain silent would be wise to remember what Dr. King said: "Our lives begin to end the day we become silent about things that matter." He also said, "In the end, we will remember not the words of our enemies, but the silence of our friends."

One of the most common recitations I hear from Christians these days is a verse from 2 Chronicles chapter 7. However, they often take it out of context. The verse comes from a passage in the Old Testament which records King Solomon's dedication of the Temple he had built for God in Jerusalem. The ceremony had concluded with fire coming down from heaven and the glory of the Lord filled the Temple. After eight days of consecration, sacrifices and worship, Solomon sent the people back to their dwelling places. Then, the Lord appeared to Solomon in a dream and gave Solomon promises and warnings. Included was this promise: "When I shut up heaven and there is no rain, or command the locusts to devour the land, or send pestilence among My people, if My people who are called by My name will humble themselves, and pray and seek My face, and turn from their wicked ways, then I will hear from heaven, and will forgive their sin and heal their land."[252] This is a conditional promise from God, an "if – then" statement. To receive the promise, the "then" clause; God's people must do three things: "humble themselves," "pray and seek" God's face, and "turn from <u>their</u> wicked ways." Many Christians in America are praying for revival, but they are not humbling themselves and turning from their wicked ways and they wonder why revival has not come. Repentance, personal and corporate, is what God is looking for from His people in America.

Every awakening in church history has had two things in common – The Word of God in the hands of the people and prayer in the hearts of the people. In 1857 there were 30,000 men idle on the streets of New York City. Drunkenness was rampant, and the nation was divided by slavery. Financial panic had hit – banks failed, railroads went bankrupt, factories closed, unemployment increased. In lower Manhattan, a Dutch Reformed Church had been steadily losing members, so they hired a layman named Jeremiah Lanphier to reverse the trend with an active visitation program. Despite his visits, church members were listless.

So, he rented a hall on Fulton Street and advertised the start of prayer meetings. On September 23, 1857, he held his first meeting, and out of a city of one million people, six people showed up a half hour late. The next week twenty-three people showed up, the following week, forty – then, on October 10th, the stock market crashed. Within six months 10,000 people were gathering daily for prayer in New York City alone. Thus, the small prayer meeting led to the Third Great Awakening. This was the first revival beginning in America with a worldwide impact. The revival spread to Ireland, Scotland, Wales, England, Europe, South Africa, India, Australia, and the Pacific Islands. As James Buchanan of Scotland summarized, it was a time when "new spiritual life was imparted to the dead, and new spiritual health imparted to the living."

We must acknowledge that success in our endeavors is not guaranteed. Like Hananiah, Mishael, and Azariah (better known by their Babylonian names – Shadrach, Meshach, and Abednego) who when threatened by King Nebuchadnezzar – they answered:

"If that is the case, our God whom we serve is able to deliver us from the burning fiery furnace, and He will deliver us from your hand, O king. But if not, let it be known to you, O king, that we do not serve your gods, nor will we worship the gold image which you have set up."[253] The King was so infuriated by their refusal to compromise and comply that he had them thrown into the fiery furnace, and while in the furnace, Jesus was with them. The king saw the Lord and was convinced that the God of these three young men was indeed the living God. Like these three, we may not be able to avoid the fiery furnace. But their courage demonstrates that it is not necessary for us to win our battles to be faithful to our calling. Peter Marshall, Pastor and twice elected as Chaplain of the US Senate said, "It is better to fail in a cause that will ultimately succeed, than to succeed in a cause that will ultimately fail." Or as missionary Jim Elliot said before he died a martyr's death: "A man is no fool to give up that which he cannot keep to gain that which he cannot lose."

CONCLUSION

It is my sincere hope that you are now able to see the world in 3-D –
looking at deception, delusion, and deliverance through the lens of
truth provided by the Holy Spirit. First, we discovered deception
is ancient and rampant everywhere today. And so, God sends
delusion. But before it is too late, we need to remember that there
is deliverance. Currently, there is deliverance for all who will call
upon the name of the Lord and place their faith in Jesus Christ.
Deliverance from deception presently, and soon and very soon,
deliverance from the delusion God will send upon humanity and
deliverance from this evil world as the shout of the archangel and
the trump of God calls us up to heaven and deliverance for Israel
as God takes them through seven terrible years of Tribulation
and deliverance for the Gentiles as the faithful remnant of Israel
preach the gospel worldwide and multitudes from every nation
come to faith in Jesus Christ!

TIME IS SHORT

But time is short, and there is much work still do be done, just as
Jesus said, "I must work the works of Him who sent Me while it
is day; the night is coming when no one can work. As long as I
am in the world, I am the light of the world."[254] Remember, Jesus
passed the baton to His followers along with a warning: "You
are the salt of the earth; but if the salt loses its flavor, how shall

it be seasoned? It is then good for nothing but to be thrown out and trampled underfoot by men. You are the light of the world. A city that is set on a hill cannot be hidden. Nor do they light a lamp and put it under a basket, but on a lampstand, and it gives light to all who are in the house. Let your light so shine before men, that they may see your good works and glorify your Father in heaven."[255] I believe that the warning from Jesus is being realized today. The church in America has lost its' way and forsaken and abdicated its' role as a preserving influence in our nation and is currently being thrown out and trampled underfoot by men.

However, God has always retained a remnant, and there are a multitude of believers who reside in the USA who are constantly and continuingly praying and serving as a witness for the Lord as they shine brightly and do good works despite living in a God-forsaking, increasingly lawless and loveless culture. Jesus warned us: "And because lawlessness will abound, the love of many will grow cold. But he who endures to the end shall be saved. And this gospel of the kingdom will be preached in all the world as a witness to all the nations, and then the end will come."[256]

SATAN'S ULTIMATE OBJECTIVE

Which reminds me – Satan's ultimate objective is to silence the gospel. He knows that the gospel is "the power of God to salvation for everyone who believes, for the Jew first and also for the Gentile."[257] As it was in the beginning, deception is his main tool, and he has used it effectively throughout human history. So, it is incumbent on believers to fight the right battles and to not be distracted in the conflict. Nor should we be discouraged when it seems that Satan is winning. The weapons in our arsenal are not weak and ineffective, just as Paul admonished the believers in Corinth: "For though we walk in the flesh, we do not war according to the flesh. For the weapons of our warfare *are* not carnal but mighty in God for pulling down strongholds, casting down arguments and every high thing that exalts itself against the knowledge of God, bringing every thought into captivity to the obedience of Christ, and being ready to punish all disobedience when your obedience is fulfilled."[258]

THE BELIEVERS' STAND

While he was in prison in Rome for preaching the gospel, Paul gave final instructions to the believers in Ephesus:

> Finally, my brethren, be strong in the Lord and in the power of His might. Put on the whole armor of God, that you may be able to stand against the wiles of the devil. For we do not wrestle against flesh and blood, but against principalities, against powers, against the rulers of the darkness of this age, against spiritual *hosts* of wickedness in the heavenly *places*. Therefore take up the whole armor of God, that you may be able to withstand in the evil day, and having done all, to stand. Stand therefore, having girded your waist with truth, having put on the breastplate of righteousness, and having shod your feet with the preparation of the gospel of peace; above all, taking the shield of faith with which you will be able to quench all the fiery darts of the wicked one. And take the helmet of salvation, and the sword of the Spirit, which is the word of God; praying always with all prayer and supplication in the Spirit, being watchful to this end with all perseverance and supplication for all the saints—and for me, that utterance may be given

to me, that I may open my mouth boldly to make known the mystery of the gospel, for which I am an ambassador in chains; that in it I may speak boldly, as I ought to speak.[259]

So, how will you successfully navigate your future? What compass will you use? I suggest you try looking into the B.I.B.L.E. – "Basic Instructions Before Leaving Earth" It is God's personal love letter to you!

ENDNOTES

1   Matthew 24:3
2   Matthew 24:4,5,11,24
3   Merriam Webster Collegiate Dictionary
4   2 Corinthians 2:11
5   Genesis 3:1
6   Revelation 12:9
7   Isaiah 14:12-15
8   Ezekiel 28:11-16
9   Genesis 1:1-2
10 Isaiah 45:18
11 Genesis 3:13-14
12 Genesis 3:15
13 Matthew 16:23
14 Matthew 16:15
15 Matthew 16:16
16 Matthew 16:17
17 Genesis 3:13
18 1 Timothy 2:14
19 Romans 5:12
20 Romans 5:15
21 Romans 5:17
22 Genesis 3:1-6
23 Matthew 4:4
24 Matthew 4:7
25 Matthew 4:10
26 Psalm 119:11
27 1 John 2:15-17, 26
28 Genesis 3:7-13

29 Genesis 3:9-13

30 John 14:30

31 Psalm 19:1-4

32 Psalm 8:1-8

33 Quoted by P.M.S. Hacker – *Human Nature: The Categorical Framework* – Wiley-Blackwell, New York, NY – copyright 2010

34 C. L. Metcalf and W. P. Flint, Destructive and Useful Insects, 4th ed. (New York: McGraw-Hill, 1962), p. 24.

35 *Natalie Angier* reported by Rick Thompson/San Francisco, Time Magazine Feb. 25, 1985, p.70.) (Cited in *The Evolution of a Creationist* by Dr. Jobe Martin, pg. 39)

36 Per Duane T. Gish, Creation Scientists Answer their Critics (El Cajon: Institute for Creation Research, 1993), pp.101-104.)

37 1 Timothy 6:20-21

38 Romans 1:18-25

39 Creativity For Creationists by William Saletan - The Slate – 12/24/14

40 1 Timothy 4:1-2

41 *Replacing Darwin* by Nathaniel T. Jeanson, PhD. - page 284

42 ibid – page 284

43 Hank Hanegraaff – *The Face That Demonstrates the Farce of* Evolution – Word Publishing, Nashville, TN – copyright 1998 - pp. 102-103

44 Sir Fred Hoyle – *Continuous Creation* – BBC Radio Broadcast – 1948 – page 4 of archived script @ St. John's College, University of Cambridge

45 *A Scientist Caught Between Two Faiths: Interview with Robert Jastrow* – Christianity Today, August 6, 1982

46 Dr. Robert Jastrow - God and The Astronomers – W. W. Norton & Co. – New York, NY – copyright 1978

47 Stephen Hawking - *A Brief History of Time,* Bantam Books, New York City, New York – copyright 1988, pp. 7, 125

48 Julian Huxley - *Evolutionary Humanism* – Prometheus Books, Brooklyn, NY – Copyright 1992

49 Isaac Asimov – *The Wellsprings of Life* - Signet, New York, NY – Copyright 1961

50 Richard Dawkins, *Put Your Money on Evolution* – The New York Times - April 9, 1989, Section 7, Page 34

51 The Guardian 9/19/09

52 *The Necessity of Darwinism* - New Scientist 94 - April 15, 1982

[53] Signature in the Cell by Stephen C. Meyer on May 12, 2012, in Research and Analysis published in The Blackwell Companion to Science and Christianity

[54] David Lightsey – *Top Evolutionists Fail to Rise to Chemist's Challenge* – World Net Daily – November 23, 2023

[55] https://www.discovery.org/b/a-mousetrap-for-darwin/

[56] David Lightsey – *Top Evolutionists Fail to Rise to Chemist's Challenge* – World Net Daily – November 23, 2023

[57] Lesson 5 - *Science: What is True?* – C

[58] John 18:37

[59] John 8:31-32

[60] Donald Grey Barnhouse – *Exposition of Bible Doctrines - Romans, vol. 1: Man's Ruin* – William B. Eerdmans Publishing Co., Grand Rapids, MI – copyright 1959

[61] John 3:16-20)

[62] John 1:10-12

[63] Charles Darwin in a letter dated May 23, 1833, to his cousin, William Darwin Fox

[64] Charles Darwin - *Descent of Man and Selection in Relation to Sex* - 1871

[65] Sir Francis Galton - *Inquiries into Human Faculty and Its Development* - 1883

[66] ibid

[67] Logo from the Second International Eugenics Congress,1921 – Currell, Susan, Cogdell, Christina (2006) *Popular Eugenics: National Efficiency and American Mass Culture in the 1930s.* Ohio University Press, Athens, OH, page 203

[68] Quoted in *Tesla, Eugenics and Rationalizing Dehumanization* by Alex Knapp, Forbes online May 19, 2012

[69] Margaret Sanger- *A Plan for Peace* - Birth Control Review, April 1932, pp. 107-108.

[70] © Copyright 1996-2020, The Alan Guttmacher Institute. (www.agi-usa.org)

[71] Washington – 5/24/09 - WorldNetDaily

[72] Quoted in *Why Nancy Pelosi's Days as Speaker of the House are Numbered* by Miranda Devine – New York Post - July 27, 2021

[73] ibid

[74] Donovan, Charles and Marshall, Robert - *Blessed Are the Barren: The Social Policy of Planned Parenthood,* (Ignatius Press, 1991), pp. 17-18.

75 Thomas Huxley - *Lay Sermons, Addresses and Reviews* - D. Appleton, New York, NY – copyright 1871

76 Henry F. Osborn, Director of the American Museum of Natural History in *The Evolution of Human Races* – Natural History magazine Jan/Feb 1926

77 Sir Arthur Keith - *Evolution and Ethics* – G.P. Putnam's Sons, New York, NY - copyright 1947

78 James M. Rhodes – *The Hitler Movement* – Hoover Institution Press, Stanford, CA - copyright 1980

79 *The Descent of Man, and Selection in Relation to Sex* – Charles Darwin – John Murray Publisher, London, UK – Copyright 1871

80 Attributed to Sigmund Freud in *Lost Paper Shows Freud's Effort to Link Analysis and Evolution* – Daniel Goleman – The New York Times – Feb. 1987

81 Julian Huxley - *Evolutionary Humanism* – Prometheus Books, Brooklyn, NY – Copyright 1992

82 Romans 1:26-27

83 Ezekiel 16:49

84 Ezekiel 16:50

85 Scott Lively – *An Open Letter to Christian Leaders in America* – World Net Daily – August 19, 2014

86 1 Peter 4:17

87 1 Timothy 3:15

88 Dr. George Barna - *American Worldview Inventory 2022 – Release #6 –* Cultural Research Center – Arizona Christian University – May 24, 2022

89 ibid

90 https://www.youtube.com/watch?v=FFZIXtm_HiU&t=1241s

91 ibid

92 ibid

93 Ezekiel 3:2-6

94 Jeremiah 23:1-2

95 Acts 20:28-30

96 2 Timothy 4:3-4

97 2 Peter 2:4-9

98 Acts 17:31

99 Al Gore - *Earth in the Balance: Ecology and the Human Spirit* – Houghton Mifflin Harcourt, Boston, MA – copyright 1992

100 ibid

101 The Ages of Gaia – New York, W.W. Morton & Co. - page 208

102 *Gaia* - Scientific American 261 – December 1989 - page 35

103 The Rebirth of Nature: The Greening of Science and of God – New York, Bantam Books 1991 – page 10

104 *A New World Vision* – The Humanist XXXIX – March/April 1979 – page 35

105 Quoted in *One Hundred Years of Teaching Children Lies About America* - George Lasley – The Tennessee Star – March 5, 2019

106 Fox News online – 8/9/21

107 CNBC – 3/21/23

108 Quoted in *Countdown to Gigadeath – From AI Arms Race to Artilect War* – posted by Joe Allen – Singularity Weekly – February 11, 2023

109 interview with BBC 12/4/14

110 interview with WIRED 11/28/17

111 *Bing's AI Chat: 'I Want to Be Alive'* - NY Times – February 17, 2023

112 *AI is About to Make Social Media (Much) More Toxic* by Jonathan Haidt & Eric Schmidt – The Atlantic - May 5, 2023

113 Rob Waugh - *China plans to mass produce humanoid robots in two years – here's how experts think the tech will change the world by 2035* – The Daily Mail, UK – November 27, 2023

114 ibid

115 ibid

116 Ray Kurzweil – *The Singularity is Near* – Viking Press, New York, NY – copyright 2005 – page 7

117 Ibid – page 9

118 Ibid – page 30

119 ibid

120 *'2030 is when the merge happens,' OpenAI president tells Netanyahu of coming man-machine merger* – All Israel News – September 25, 2023

121 Genesis 47:15

122 Jefferson, Thomas. *The Works, vol. 11 (Correspondence and Papers 1808-1816)*. G. P. Putnam's Sons, 1905

123 In His Own Words: Abraham Lincoln on Banking Office of the Comptroller of the Currency CWAL, volume 5, pages 282- 83.

124 In His Own Words: Abraham Lincoln on Banking Office of the Comptroller of the Currency CWAL, volume 8, pages 143 – 44.

125 Forbes – 8/24/2023

126 Independent News UK - 8/12/11

127 Revelation 14:9-11

[128] Revelation 13:16-18

[129] Carla Norrlof – University of Toronto – 4/17/14

[130] The Daily Reckoning 1/13/17

[131] Rueters – 8/4/11)

[132] UN website: https://sustainabledevelopment.un.org/outcomedocuments/agenda21

[133] CNN – 7/8/23

[134] *Treasury just dropped a financial bomb, but Bidenomics means the worst is yet to come - The Treasury fiddles as the nation's finances burn around it* – by E. J. Antoni – Fox Business – October 25, 2023

[135] ibid

[136] ibid

[137] ibid

[138] Cicero – 63 B.C.

[139] Quoted by Trevor Thomas – *Is it About Good Samaritans or Bad Government?* – The Gainesville Times – September 21, 2011

[140] Dr. Bill Choby - *Liberty in America, Past, Present and Future: A Prescription for America* – AuthorHouse, Bloomington, IN – copyright 2010, pg 101

[141] Ann Pettifor – *Debtonation – The Coming First World Debt Crisis* – Palgrave MacMillan – London, UK – Copyright 2006

[142] Larry Burkett – *The Coming Economic Earthquake* – Moody Publishers, Chicago, IL – Copyright 1991

[143] Ezekiel 7:19

[144] R. Warren Anderson & Dan Gainor - *Fire and Ice* – Business Media Institute – May 17, 2006

[145] ibid

[146] ibid

[147] ibid

[148] ibid

[149] 2 Timothy 3:13

[150] 2 Timothy 3:14-15

[151] 1 Timothy 4:1

[152] Galatians 1:6-9

[153] 2 Timothy 3:13

[154] *Let God Be True* - page 198 - 1952 edition

[155] Matthew 24:23-24

[156] Efraim Karsh – *Islamic Imperialism – A History* – Yale University Press, New Haven, CT – Copyright 2007 – pages 10-11

[157]   Ibid – pages 212-213

[158]   Ambassador Sidi Haji Abdrahaman - March 1785

[159]   Efraim Karsh – *Islamic Imperialism – A History* – Yale University Press, New Haven, CT – Copyright 2007 – Introduction

[160]   ibid

[161]   ibid

[162]   ibid

[163]   Quoted in *Prophecy 20/20 – Profiling the Future Through the Lens of Scripture* by Chuck Missler – page 149 – Thomas Nelson, Inc, Nashville, TN – Copyright 2006

[164]   2 Thessalonians 2:9-12

[165]   John 8:44

[166]   Section 1, Chapter 27, House Bill No. 185 - Public Acts of the State of Tennessee passed by the Sixty-Fourth General Assembly, 1925

[167]   Jeffrey P. Moran – The Scopes Trial: A Brief History with Documents – Bedford/St. Martin's, Boston, MA & New York, NY – copyright 2002

[168]   2 Corinthians 11:14

[169]   *Archeology, Anthropology, and Interstellar Communications* – edited by Douglas A. Vakoch – The NASA History Series, NASA, Washington, DC – copyright 2014 - page 17

[170]   Quoted by Lee Dye in article - *Scientists Ponder Earthlings' Reactions: If There Is Life on Other Planets, What Do We Do?* – Los Angeles Times, Los Angeles, CA – October 16, 1987

[171]   Lee Dye - *Scientists Ponder Earthlings' Reactions: If There Is Life on Other Planets, What Do We Do?* – Los Angeles Times, Los Angeles, CA – October 16, 1987

[172]   Isaiah 66:4

[173]   Amos 8:11-12

[174]   Psalm 119:105

[175]   Deut. 28:20, 28-29a

[176]   *Newsboys Co-founder Denounces Christianity: 'I'm Now an Atheist'* - Jennifer Laclaire - Charisma News – January 23, 2015

[177]   Quoted in *Vicky Beeching, Christian Rock Star 'I'm Gay. God loves me just the way I am'* – Patrick Strudwick – The Independent US Edition – August 14, 2014

[178]   *Why Are So Many Christians Turning Into Atheists?* – Jennifer Laclaire - Charisma News 1/2/15

[179]   Matthew 24:12

[180]   1 Timothy 4:1-2

181   Revelation 17:1, 7
182   Revelation 17:5
183   Genesis 10:8-10
184   Jeremiah 7:18
185   Jeremiah 44:25
186   Ezekiel 8:14
187   Matthew 13:13
188   Zechariah 5:5-11)
189
190   Nahum 3:4
191   James 4:4
192   Revelation 18:4-5
193   Revelation 17:7-8
194   Revelation 17:7-8
195   Psalm 30:7
196   Daniel 2:35
197   Winston Churchill – *speech delivered at the University of Zurich 19 September 1946* - Council of Europe - https://rm.coe.int/16806981f3
198   Revelation 17:13
199   David Jeremiah- *What in the World is Going On? - 10 Prophetic Clues You Cannot Afford to Ignore* – Thomas Nelson, Nashville, TN - copyright 2010
200   Quoted by Mark Hitchcock – The End of Money-Prophecy and the Coming Economic Collapse – Harvest House Publishers, Eugene, OR – copyright 2013, page 104
201   International Herald Tribune – 1/12/2009
202   2 Thessalonians 2:3-8
203   Revelation 17:15-17
204   Matthew 23:37-39
205   Acts 2:16-21
206   John 14:16-17
207   John 16:8
208   John 16:9-11
209   John 3:18
210   John 3:36
211   Hebrews 10:29-31
212   Colossians 2:14-15
213   John 14:26
214   John 16:12-13

215 2 Corinthians 1:9-10
216 Colossians 1:13-14
217 Galatians 1:3-4
218 1 Thessalonians 1:9-10
219 John 8:12
220 John 8:31,36
221 John 14:6
222 John 18:38
223 2 Thess. 2:7
224 Acts 2:19-20
225 https://themayflowersociety.org/history/the-mayflower-compact/
226 https://encyclopediavirginia.org/entries/first-charter-of-virginia-1606/
227 Zephaniah 1:14-18
228 Gregory M. Davis - *Religion of Peace? Islam's War Against the World* – World Ahead Publishing – copyright 2006
229 Jeremiah 25:15-16
230 Jerry Gordon - *How the CIA Helped The Muslim Brotherhood Infiltrate the West* – New English Review, Nashville, TN – posted August 2011
231 ibid
232 ibid
233 *An Explanatory Memorandum on the General Strategic Goal for the Group in North America* – May 12, 2011
234 Hauser, Albrecht. 2012. *Da'wah: Islamic Mission and its Current Implications* - International Bulletin of Missionary Research Vol. 36 (4): P. 189-194.)
235 Zephaniah 2:1-3
236 Zephaniah 2:4,8
237 Acts 2:17-21
238 Joel 2:32b
239 Acts 15:13-18
240 Jeremiah 30:7
241 Malachi 4:5-6
242 Acts 15:17)
243 Amos 9:11
244 Ezekiel 39:23-24
245 Ezekiel 39:29
246 Joel 2:23
247 Romans 11:25-27

[248] Numbers 6:22-27
[249] Jeremiah 18:1-12
[250] Isaiah 40:15,17
[251] The Truth Project – Focus on the Family, Colorado Springs, CO – copyright 2007
[252] 2 Chronicles 7:13-14
[253] Daniel 3:17-18
[254] John 9:4-5
[255] Matthew 5:13-16
[256] Matthew 24:12-14
[257] Romans 1:16
[258] 2 Corinthians 10:3-6
[259] Ephesians 6:10-20

BIBLIOGRAPHY

BOOKS -

Donald Grey Barnhouse – *The Invisible War* – Zondervan Publishing House, Grand Rapids, MI – Copyright 1965

Warren W. Wiersbe – *The Strategy of Satan – How to Detect and Defeat Him* – Tyndale House Publishers, Inc., Wheaton, IL – Copyright 1979

Walter Martin- *The Maze of Mormonism* – Zondervan Publishing House, Grand Rapids, MI – Copyright 1962

Walter Martin- *The Kingdom of the Cults* – Bethany House – Bloomington, MN – Copyright 1965

John Morris and Steven A. Austin. *Footprints in the Ash – The Explosive Story of Mount St. Helens* – Master Books, Green Forest, AR – Copyright 2003

Michael J. Behe. *Darwin's Black Box – The Biochemical Challenge to Evolution* - The Free Press, New York, NY – Copyright 1996

Ray Rempt. *Big Bang to Kingdom Come – Creator, Creature, and Creation in Perspective* – Fig Tree Publications

Hank Hanegraaff – *The Face That Demonstrates the Farce of Evolution* – Word Publishing, Nashville, TN – Copyright 1998

A.E. Wilder-Smith – *The Scientific Alternative to Neo-Darwinian Evolutionary Theory* – The Word for Today Publishers, Costa Mesa, CA – Copyright 1987

A.E. Wilder-Smith – *The Natural Sciences Know Nothing of Evolution* – The Word for Today Publishers, Costa Mesa, CA – Copyright 1981

Dr. Don DeYoung – *Thousands…Not Billions – Challenging an Icon of Evolution – Questioning the Age of the Earth* - Master Books, Green Forest, AR – Copyright 2005

Tom DeRosa – *Evolution's Fatal Fruit – How Darwin's Tree of Life Brought Death to Millions* – Coral Ridge Ministries, Fort Lauderdale, FL – Copyright 2006

Jonathan Cahn – *The Mystery of the Shemitah* – FrontLine, Lake Mary, FL – Copyright 2014

Alan Sears & Craig Osten – *The Homosexual Agenda-Exposing the Principal Threat to Religious Liberty Today* – Broadman & Holman Publishers, Nashville, TN – Copyright 2003

Peter Sprigg – *Outrage-How Gay Activists and Liberal Judges are Trashing Democracy to Redefine Marriage* – Regnery Publishing, Inc., Washington, DC – Copyright 2004

Eric D. Saxon – *Covenant of Shadows (The Dark Promise)* – The Kodel Group, Grants Pass, OR – Copyright 2014

Ken Ham & Britt Beemer with Todd Hillard – *Already Gone – Why Your Kids Will Quit Church and What You Can Do to Stop It* - Master Books, Green Forest, AR – Copyright 2009

Josh McDowell – *The Last Christian Generation* – Green Key Books, Holiday, FL – Copyright 2006

Douglas Hamp – *Corrupting the Image – Angels, Aliens, and the Antichrist Revealed* – Copyright 2011

Neil Postman - *Technopoly: The Surrender of Culture to Technology* – Vintage – Copyright 1993

Ann Pettifor – *Debtonation – The Coming First World Debt Crisis* – Palgrave MacMillan – London, UK – Copyright 2006

Larry Burkett – *The Coming Economic Earthquake* – Moody Publishers, Chicago, IL – Copyright 1991

Nathaniel T. Jeanson – *Replacing Darwin – The New Origin of Species* - Master Books, Green Forest, AR – Copyright 2017

Mark Biltz – *Blood Moons – Decoding the Imminent Heavenly Signs* – WND Books, Washington, DC – Copyright 2014

Jim Telow, Roger Oakland, Brad Meyers– *Queen of Rome, Queen of Islam, Queen of All – The Marian apparitions' plan to unite all religions under the Roman Catholic Church* - Eternal Productions, Fairport, NY – Copyright 2006

John C. Whitcomb and Henry M. Morris – *The Genesis Flood – The Biblical Record and its Scientific Implications* - Baker Books, Grand Rapids, MI – Copyright 1961

Walid Shoebat and Joel Richardson – *God's War on Terror – Islam, Prophecy, and the Bible* – Top Executive Media – Copyright 2008

Ian Johnson – *A Mosque in Munich - Nazis, the CIA, and the Rise of the Muslim Brotherhood in the West* – Mariner Books, Boston, MA – Copyright 2011

Ramon Bennett – *Philistine – The Great Deception* – Shekinah Books, Citrus Heights, CA – Copyright 1995

Rabbi Yechiel Weitzman – *The Ishmaelite Exile* – Jerusalem Publications, Jerusalem, Israel – Copyright 2006

William J. Federer – *What Every American Needs to Know About the Quran – a History of Islam & the United States* – Amerisearch, Inc., St. Louis, MO – Copyright 2007

Erick Stakelbeck – *The Brotherhood – America's Next Great Enemy* – Regnery Publishing, Washington, DC – Copyright 2013

Efraim Karsh – *Islamic Imperialism – A History* – Yale University Press, New Haven, CT – Copyright 2007

Hal Lindsay – *The Everlasting Hatred – The Roots of Jihad* – Oracle House Publishing, Murrieta, CA – Copyright 2002

Don Richardson – *Secrets of the Koran* – Regal Books, Ventura, CA – Copyright 2003

Chuck Missler - *Prophecy 20/20 – Profiling the Future Through the Lens of Scripture* - Thomas Nelson, Inc, Nashville, TN – Copyright 2006

David Leeming and Jake Page - *Goddess: Myths of the Female Divine* - Oxford University Press, Oxford, UK – Copyright 1996

Erwin W. Lutzer – *When a Nation Forgets God – 7 Lessons We Must Learn from Nazi Germany* – Moody Publishers, Chicago, IL – Copyright 2016

David Barton – *The Jefferson Lies: Exposing the Myths You've Always Believed About Thomas Jefferson* – Thomas Nelson, Inc, Nashville, TN – copyright 2012

PAMPHLETS -

Timothy J. Daily – *The Bible, the Church & Homosexuality – Exposing the 'Gay' Theology* – Family Research Council, Washington, DC – Copyright 2004

Henry M. Morris – *Some Call It Science – the Religion of Evolution* – Institute For Creation Research, Santee, CA – Copyright 2006

Lee C. Ryker – *A Scientist's Discussion of Evolution* – Jacksonville, OR – Copyright 2006

Larry Vardiman – *A New Theory of Climate Change* - Institute For Creation Research, Dallas, TX – Copyright 2009

VIDEOS -

Icons of Evolution – ColdWater Media, Palmer Lake, CO – Copyright 2010

Incredible Creatures That Defy Evolution – 1 & 2 – Exploration Films

Expelled- No Intelligence Allowed – Premise Media Corporation – Copyright 2008

Creation and the Last Days – Answers In Genesis – Copyright 2014

Jihad I America – The Grand Deception – SAE Productions – Copyright 2012

ABOUT THE AUTHOR

 "Tune in, turn on, drop out." That phrase rang out in the 1960's as youth's desperate cry of frustration and despair. Denny Stahl knew the despair and pain of drug addiction until he tuned in and was turned on to the solution to life's emptiness: a personal relationship with Jesus Christ. That was in 1969, early in the so-called Jesus Movement among young people throughout the world during the turbulent years of Vietnam and the Hippie sub-culture. "Where sin abounded, grace overflowed".

A talented musician, vocalist, and composer, Denny ministered as a solo artist with Maranatha! Music during its infancy.

Denny was ordained as a pastor by the Applegate Christian Fellowship in 1984, and served in that capacity in several churches, most recently as the Senior Pastor of Calvary Chapel Grants Pass until 2018, when he became the Regional Manager in the Pacific Northwest for the Billy Graham Evangelistic Association. Denny is now enjoying retirement and busy writing manuscripts for publication.

Since 2005, Denny has also served as a volunteer for Family Research Council, representing their Watchmen on the Wall initiative in the State of Oregon. Tony Perkins, President of

Family Research Council, began the Watchmen on the Wall initiative to champion pastors to transform America.

Denny also served as Oregon State Director for Christians United For Israel 2011 - 2018. Since its humble beginning in 1992 as a meeting of 400 Christian leaders in San Antonio, Texas, Christians United for Israel has grown to 12 million members, the largest pro-Israel organization of its kind.

Denny and his wife of 39 years, Vickie, reside in a small town in Oregon and have three grown children and seven grandchildren.

Printed in the United States
by Baker & Taylor Publisher Services